JENNIFER CHIAVERINI

more ELM CREEK QUILTS

30+ Traditional Blocks • 11 Projects • Favorite Character Sketches

C&T PUBLISHING

Text copyright © 2008 by Jennifer Chiaverini

Artwork copyright © 2008 by C&T Publishing, Inc.

Publisher: Amy Marson

Editorial Director: Gailen Runge

Acquisitions Editor: Jan Grigsby

Editors: Karla Menaugh and Kesel Wilson

Technical Editors: Wendy Mathson, Rebekah Genz, and Carolyn Aune

Copyeditor/Proofreader: Wordfirm Inc.

Cover Designer: Kristen Yenche

Book Designer: Rose Sheifer-Wright

Production Coordinator: Tim Manibusan

Illustrator: Wendy Mathson

Photography by Luke Mulks and Diane Pedersen of C&T Publishing unless otherwise noted Published by C&T Publishing, Inc., P.O. Box 1456, Lafayette, CA 94549.

Title page photo by Rose Sheifer-Wright.

Library of Congress Cataloging-in-Publication Data

Chiaverini, Jennifer.
  More Elm Creek quilts : 30+ traditional blocks, 11 projects, favorite character sketches / Jennifer Chiaverini.
    p. cm.
  Quilt projects from several novels in the Elm Creek series, with sidebars about characters pertinent to each quilt, with specially written vignettes and a chapter contained only in this book.
  ISBN 978-1-57120-451-6 (paper trade : alk. paper)
  1. Patchwork--Patterns. 2. Quilting--Patterns. 3. Patchwork quilts. I. Title.

TT835.C4555 2008
746.46'041--dc22

2007025265

Printed in China
10 9 8 7 6 5 4 3 2 1

Dedication

To all Elm Creek Readers and quilters who use their talents to make the world a better place.

Acknowledgments

This book would not have been possible without the guidance of my editors, Karla Menaugh and Kesel Wilson, the wonderful people at C&T Publishing, and the generous Elm Creek Readers who sent in Chimneys and Cornerstones blocks for the *Lucinda's Gift* quilt. Thank you, one and all.

I am deeply grateful to Denise Roy, Maria Massie, and Rebecca Davis for their countless contributions to the Elm Creek Quilts novels through the years.

Many thanks to Tara Shaughnessy, nanny extraordinaire, who cares for my boys and gives me time to write.

Thank you to the friends and family who continue to support and encourage me, especially Geraldine Neidenbach, Heather Neidenbach, Nic Neidenbach, Virginia Riechman, and Leonard and Marlene Chiaverini.

Most of all, I am grateful to my husband, Marty, and my sons, Nicholas and Michael, for everything.

Contents

The Spirit of *Elm Creek Quilts* 4

From *The Sugar Camp Quilt* 7
    Authors' Album 10
    Constance's Marriage Quilt 14
    The Sugar Camp Quilt 18

From *The Christmas Quilt* 26
    Christmas Memories 28
    Christmas Greetings From Elm Creek Manor 35

From *Circle of Quilters* 55
    Violets for Gretchen 57
    Mill Girls 62

From *The Quilter's Homecoming* 65
    Lucinda's Gift 67
    Road to Triumph Ranch 71
    Arboles Valley Star 74

From *The New Year's Quilt* 78
    New Year's Reflections 80

Quilting 101 88

About the Author 93

About the Quiltmakers 93

Resources 95

THE SPIRIT OF
Elm Creek Quilts

Jennifer Chiaverini addressing *Elm Creek Quilts* fans at the Lancaster Heritage Quilt Show, 2005.

When I wrote the first Elm Creek Quilts novel in 1996, I never dreamed that through the years, my stories would come to inspire so many people around the world to make positive changes in their lives and their communities. Some readers, who identified with Sarah McClure's uncertainty in a new town, followed her example and joined local quilting guilds to build new friendships. Others, moved by Sylvia Compson's lost opportunities to reconcile with her estranged sister, mended broken relationships within their own families. One woman found inspiration in the story of Grace Daniels, whose multiple sclerosis made quilting a challenge. Contending with the same illness, my reader decided that, like Grace, she would find a way to continue the work that she loved, teaching elementary school. So many readers like this amazing Wisconsin schoolteacher have shared their own stories with me, at book signings and quilt shows, through letters and emails. Each story is a gift I receive with gratitude.

These determined and compassionate readers often remind me of Dorothea Granger, the heroine of *The Sugar Camp Quilt*, who sewed an opportunity quilt autographed by prominent authors of her era to raise money to build a library in her small, rural town. I made a version of the *Authors' Album* quilt as a fundraiser for the Candlelighters Childhood Cancer Foundation, but I was not the only one inspired by Dorothea's project.

Terri Sconfienza from Wilkes-Barre, Pennsylvania, discovered the *Elm Creek Quilts* novels when she purchased *The Christmas Quilt* as a Christmas gift for her mother.

Their own quilting lessons had seen them through a challenging time. A few years before, Terri's mother had lived with her as she underwent treatment for cancer. Terri's mother, missing her own home and her husband, passed the time by teaching Terri how to quilt. Before long Terri knew how to quilt—and she and her mother had read the entire *Elm Creek Quilts* series. "When I read Dorothea Granger's idea of making an *Authors' Album* opportunity quilt to raise the funds needed to build a public library in *The Sugar Camp Quilt*," Terri wrote to me, "I immediately knew I had to make one." During her mother's treatment, Terri had met many other cancer patients, some of whom were less fortunate than her own family. "Many people have jobs that provide inadequate or no medical coverage at all, or they are self-employed," Terri said. "Sometimes their insurance won't cover a treatment that is their best course of action or won't cover a drug because it comes in a pill form rather than an IV infusion." Determined to help, Terri decided to make a signature raffle quilt to benefit the Medical Oncology Associates (MOA) Prescription Assistance Fund, a nonprofit foundation created to help financially disadvantaged cancer patients obtain prescription medications and supplements essential to their treatment. At the time that I write this, Terri is still working on her quilt, collecting signatures and piecing blocks, but she expects to have it finished soon so that the MOA can raffle it off in 2007. "Aside from the physical and emotional effects, cancer can be devastating financially," Terri pointed out. "Many patients must miss

Anne Spurgeon, director of Capital Candlelighters, with the original *Authors' Album* quilt.

Best-selling author Jennifer Weiner and the *Authors' Album* quilt, in progress.

work due to their illness, which negatively impacts their ability to pay their bills and take care of their families." Terri is helping the MOA ease those worries so that local cancer patients can focus on their treatment and recovery.

Like Terri, the 65 members of an unusual book club were also inspired by Dorothea's project. The Great Escape Book Club, sponsored by the Education Department at the Robert Ellsworth Correctional Center in Union Grove, Wisconsin, promotes literacy and the love of reading among the inmates at the minimum-security women's facility. The program also aims to prepare the women for reintegration into society by encouraging them to think beyond themselves and give back to the community. While reading *The Quilter's Apprentice*, the women became intrigued by the traditional art form, and they decided to make their own *Authors' Album* quilt. The book club members eventually received 37 signatures in the mail—including autographs from Bill Cosby, Sue Grafton, and Judy Blume—which they pieced into blocks and sewed together with yellow sashing and green borders. The quilt raffle raised $2,016 to benefit the Racine Literacy Council, Cops-N-Kids, and the Racine Public Library Foundation. The women also discovered a new love for quilting, which some of the inmates have said they will share with their children upon their release.

As the members of the Great Escape Book Club learned, quilting fosters community. Several *Elm Creek Quilts* internet communities have come about because of my second pattern book, *Return to Elm Creek*, which included patterns for five six-inch blocks from *Sylvia's Bridal Sampler*, a 140-block sampler described in my sixth novel,

Acclaimed author Chang-Rae Lee signs a patch for Jennifer's *Authors' Album* quilt.

The Master Quilter. Readers were so pleased with the five blocks that in October 2005 I created a new website where quilters could download the remaining patterns. Quilters posted their comments—and corrections, to the benefit of all—and emailed photos of their completed blocks, which are proudly displayed in a virtual gallery. The Sylvia's Bridal Sampler (SBS) Quilters encourage one another, celebrate their accomplishments, and participate in block swaps on a mailing list. They also support one another in times of crisis. In the summer of 2006, when an SBS Quilter nicknamed Bunny suffered a serious health condition, the other quilters rallied around her, expressing their thoughts and prayers in signature blocks. I like to think that our prayers and good wishes lifted her spirits and helped speed her recovery.

Fans at a book signing

Photos by Patsy McCluskey

Martin and Patsy McCluskey at the Homestead Cabin Retreat.

The interest in *Sylvia's Bridal Sampler* quilts has spread beyond my own website to other, independent online communities. Dutch quilter Annelies van den Bergh sponsors her own mailing list for other Dutch quilters inspired to make their own quilts. German quilter Heike Jesse manages a website for the members of her quilting circle, the Quiltfriends, where they post images of their quilts in progress and exchange advice and support. But not all *Sylvia's Bridal Sampler* groups meet online. Reader Elise Fare wrote to tell me about the Maxwell Branch Library Second Saturday Quilting Bees, a group of quilters in Jacksonville, Florida, who are working on their samplers together. Elise, an employee of the library and an experienced quilter, set up the program when she heard that aspiring quilters in the area were interested in taking lessons. The Bees are a mix of beginners and more experienced quilters, Elise explained, adding, "The beginners are getting instructions and those with experience teach and assist the beginners." When Elise's *Sylvia's Bridal Sampler* is complete, the quilters plan to display it in the library for a time to thank the library for providing their group with a place to meet.

The Second Saturday Quilting Bees understand that quilters need places to gather, a lesson that resonated with Wisconsin quilter Patsy McCluskey. While reading *The Quilter's Apprentice* on the porch swing of an 1850s log cabin that she and her husband had recently renovated, she reflected upon Sylvia and Sarah's preparations for the arrival of a new group of quilt campers. "I took inspiration from Jennifer Chiaverini's book and realized I now had a

new passion," Patsy explained, "a dream to create a place where for a moment, women were sure to be surrounded by a creative environment, an inspirational setting, and a place where they could relax. I believe I have created such a place."

I imagine Sylvia and Sarah would agree. "Most of my guests bring their own projects to work on rather than having a class-filled weekend like Elm Creek Manor," Patsy said, "but quilters find respite at the Homestead Cabin Retreat and I believe they return to their jobs inspired and refreshed with new ideas—and the satisfaction of completing what they set out to accomplish." Her guests' glowing testimonials concur. Patsy framed an autographed book jacket from *The Quilter's Apprentice* and proudly displays it in the main workroom of her quilters' haven, and I am honored to think that my books played a role in Patsy's remarkable achievement.

As I put the finishing touches on a new novel and a third pattern book, I wonder what inspiration readers and quilters will find within the pages. *More Elm Creek Quilts* offers fans of the *Elm Creek Quilts* series eleven new quilts sure to evoke fond memories of hours spent at Elm Creek Manor with Sylvia, Sarah, and their Circle of Quilters. I invite you to try your hand at these new projects and I welcome you to share your own quilting accomplishments with me. I hope that these quilt patterns—and the inspiring stories of the friendships forged and good works done by other Elm Creek quilters in their communities— will encourage you to make your own world a better place, piece by lovingly sewn piece.

FROM *THE SUGAR CAMP QUILT*

In *The Sugar Camp Quilt*, set in Creek's Crossing, Pennsylvania, in the years leading up to the Civil War, friends and neighbors are taking sides in the national debate over abolition. When Dorothea Granger and the most prominent ladies in town sew an opportunity quilt signed by famous authors to raise money to build a library, the mayor's wife, Violet Pearson Engle, rejects several of Dorothea's favorite authors because of their abolitionist writings. Dorothea's project inspired me to create an *Authors' Album* opportunity quilt for Capital Candlelighters, the Madison, Wisconsin, branch of the Candlelighters Childhood Cancer Foundation. Capital Candlelighters is a nonprofit organization serving families whose children have been diagnosed with cancer, especially those treated at the University of Wisconsin Children's Hospital. Thanks to the 61 generous authors and quilters who signed patches for the quilt, Capital Candlelighters raised thousands of dollars to support young cancer patients and their families.

A friend who shares Dorothea's abolitionist beliefs is Constance Wright, the young bride of Abel, a freeman who purchased her freedom from a Virginia slaveholder. While still enslaved, Constance saved her mistress's discarded scraps of fabric. When Abel asked her to marry him, she secretly sewed the scraps into a beautiful string-pieced star wedding quilt, placing her faith in Abel's love and in his vow to bring her to freedom in the North.

Dorothea makes *The Sugar Camp Quilt* at the request of her stern Uncle Jacob, who sketches a Delectable Mountains variation with several unusual blocks of his own design. Only after her uncle's death does Dorothea discover that the quilt includes secret clues to guide fugitive slaves along the Underground Railroad to freedom in the North. To evoke the era, I used my reproduction fabric line, *Gerda's Collection* from Red Rooster Fabrics.

The Sugar Camp Quilt is a work of fiction. The debate about the role of quilts as signals on the Underground Railroad is ongoing, with the oral tradition often at odds with documented historical fact. In my novels, I have tried to remain faithful to the historical record while also presenting a plausible explanation for the evolution of the legend. To learn more about this controversy, please see Barbara Brackman's *Facts and Fabrications: Unraveling the History of Quilts and Slavery* by C&T Publishing.

Dorothea Granger

In 1849, nineteen-year-old Dorothea Granger lives with her parents on her Uncle Jacob's farm, her dreams of furthering her education in an eastern city thwarted by the needs of home. She briefly serves as the teacher of the Creek's Crossing school and is disappointed when she loses the job to the privileged son of a local benefactor. A passionate reader, Dorothea initiates a campaign to raise funds for a library and unexpectedly finds herself at odds with some of the town's most prominent ladies. She is devoted to suffragist and abolitionist causes, courageously risking her own life to protect fugitive slaves fleeing north along the Underground Railroad.

Jacob Kuehner

Uncle Jacob's stern demeanor conceals deep religious convictions and a commitment to justice even from those closest to him. Under his strict leadership, the Kuehner farm prospers and his sugar camp gains fame for producing the best maple sugar in the county. When he inexplicably asks Dorothea to stitch him a quilt with unusual patterns of his own design, she reluctantly complies, never suspecting that her uncle is a stationmaster on the Underground Railroad or that the mysterious quilt contains hidden clues to guide runaway slaves to freedom.

Photo by Jennifer Chiaverini.

Son Michael gives *The Sugar Camp Quilt* his seal of approval.

Thomas Nelson

The son of a beloved local benefactor, Thomas Nelson returns to Creek's Crossing to take over management of the family farm—and Dorothea's teaching position—amidst rumors that he has been banished to Creek's Crossing after suffering a near fatal illness in prison. Aloof and taciturn, he earns Dorothea's enmity by taking her job and criticizing her and the other young ladies of the town, unaware that Dorothea is listening nearby. As time passes, Dorothea learns the truth about his questionable past, and discovers that he is a better man than she ever suspected.

Violet Pearson Engle

As the mayor's wife, Violet Pearson Engle considers herself the leader of the town's women and the authority in all matters of propriety and taste. Proud, vain, and scheming, she places her own family's well being and prosperity above all other considerations but is careful to make it appear as if she is acting for the common good. On the issue of slavery, Violet sympathizes with southern slaveholders, and believes that instead of casting their own ballots, women should endeavor to exert moral influence on their sons and husbands and nothing more. Her positions—and her attempts to force others to accept them—create tension between Violet and Dorothea.

Cyrus Pearson

Violet Pearson Engle's grown son from her first marriage has recently returned to Creek's Crossing after six months abroad. Handsome, witty, and charming, he courts Dorothea, but although she enjoys his company, she is sometimes exasperated by his unwillingness to take anything seriously. Through no fault of Dorothea's, Cyrus mistakenly believes that she will inherit her uncle's farm upon his death. Upon discovering the truth, he abruptly shifts his attention to another girl of more certain fortune, forcing Dorothea to consider that she may have misjudged not only Cyrus, but other men in her life as well.

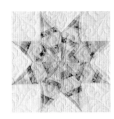

Constance Wright

A former slave, Constance comes to Creek's Crossing after her husband, Abel, purchases her freedom from a Virginia plantation. Understandably wary of white strangers, Constance initially rejects Dorothea's offers of friendship but over time comes to trust her. Constance is staunchly loyal to her husband, and knowing the sacrifices he made to bring her to freedom, she rightly never doubts his love for her.

With an indulgent smile, Mrs. Engle turned and made her way toward the quilt frame. The crowd parted before the formidable woman and closed just as quickly behind her so Dorothea was forced to dodge passersby and groups gathered in conversation. She tried to call out to Mrs. Engle, but her voice was lost in the din.

When she finally caught up to Mrs. Engle, she was standing rigid and wide-eyed at the side of the quilt frame. Two other women had joined the original six, and already they had completed a significant portion of the quilt with meticulous, feathery quilting.

Mrs. Engle did not even turn to look at her. "What is the meaning of this?"

"I meant to tell you—"

"As you should have done!" Two spots of red appeared in the plump ivory of Mrs. Engle's cheeks. "I distinctly recall stating that this man—" She jabbed a finger at one block. "—And this man—" The finger again pointed accusingly. "Were not suitable for this quilt!"

The quilters looked up cautiously but did not pause in their work. Dorothea took a deep breath. "You did indeed tell me that, but I thought—"

"You thought?" Mrs. Engle trembled with anger and disbelief, her powdered jowls shaking from the effort of controlling her temper. "You were not placed on the library board to think. You were included because we thought your uncle might make a donation on your behalf!"

Dorothea could not imagine why they had thought such a thing. "I regret that you were disappointed in that regard," she said. "However, you did include me, and therefore I was obligated to do my very best to make this fund-raiser a success. While you do not care for these authors, their works are widely read and respected in the community, and thus their inclusion increases the value of the quilt."

"You do not know the reading habits of our community very well if you believe that," retorted Mrs. Engle.

—Excerpted from *The Sugar Camp Quilt* by Jennifer Chiaverini

As her mother went to the kitchen, Dorothea found the bedroom but lingered in the doorway, studying the quilt already spread upon the bed. It was an unusual string-pieced star pattern, one Dorothea had never seen before, probably stitched from the leftover scraps or even remnants of older quilts.

"Dorothea?" Lorena joined her in the doorway, and spotted the quilt that had captured Dorothea's attention. "Perhaps you should place the appliqué sampler over it."

"Why?" The fabric in the quilt did not appear to be new, but the colors had held fast, the stitches were small and even, and the binding was not worn. Perhaps the quilt had been made more recently than it appeared. "I think it's rather striking."

"Yes, but it is not quite the thing for a bridal chamber."

Dorothea thought of the elaborately pieced, appliquéd, and stuffed creations some of her friends had made as their own nuptials approached, beautiful, decorative, and often too fine for daily use. Her best friend and her husband, married only seven months, had last slept beneath their quilt on their wedding night, although Mary was considering releasing it from the hope chest for their first anniversary. In comparison, Abel Wright's quilt was less lovely and impressive, but far more comfortable and enduring. She wondered how he had come to own it. He did not piece quilts himself, as far as she knew.

"Perhaps it is not a proper bridal quilt," said Dorothea. "But is a perfect marriage quilt."

—Excerpted from *The Sugar Camp Quilt* by Jennifer Chiaverini

"I assume you mean for me to fill in these blank places with light-colored fabric?" [Dorothea] inquired, indicating a diagonal row of squares from the upper left corner to the center of the quilt in his illustration. In an ordinary Delectable Mountains quilt, those squares would have been part of larger triangles of background fabric.

"Do no more and no less than you are told," said Uncle Jacob. "I'll need more time to sketch those squares. Make the part of the quilt I have drawn first and do the rest later."

Delicately, because her uncle had clearly given his design a great deal of thought, she said, "It will be difficult to assemble the rest of the quilt with these important blocks missing, especially the center. Perhaps I should wait until you have completed your drawing."

"I've watched you sew," her uncle retorted. "I've seen how long it takes you to stitch two little triangles together. If you wait until my drawing is done, you'll never finish the quilt in time."

Dorothea managed to keep from sighing. "Very well," she said. "What colors would you like?"

"Serviceable colors. Whatever scraps you have in your sewing basket will be fine."

"You have said nothing about how large you would like your quilt to be."

"The usual size will do."

Abruptly as that, he departed for the barn, calling over his shoulder for Dorothea's father. Dorothea watched the men go, mystified. A quiltmaker would never spend so much time on a design for a quilt only to dismiss qualities as important as color and size. Of course, Uncle Jacob was no quiltmaker, despite the care he had lavished on his drawing, or he would have known it was no simple matter to leave empty spaces in a quilt top to fill in later. Perhaps he did know, but did not mind the extra work and difficulty it created, since he was not the one to sew it.

—Excerpted from *The Sugar Camp Quilt* by Jennifer Chiaverini

AUTHORS' ALBUM

From *The Sugar Camp Quilt* by Jennifer Chiaverini

FINISHED SIZE: 76″ × 76″
FINISHED BLOCK SIZE: 8″ × 8″
NUMBER OF BLOCKS: 61
Machine pieced by Jennifer Chiaverini, machine quilted by Sue Vollbrecht, 2005.

FABRIC REQUIREMENTS

- **Print fabrics in dark greens, plums, wines, and golds:** ½ yard each of 16 fabrics
- **Light beige:** ¾ yard (for signature patches)
- **Beige:** 5½ yards (includes binding)
- **Batting:** 80″ × 80″
- **Backing:** 4½ yards

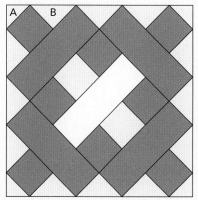

CUTTING

The featured border requires advanced sewing skills. Feel free to substitute a simpler border. (**Note:** scant means 1 or 2 thread widths less than a full measurement.

Dark prints

- Cut 4 squares 2⅝″ for the border.
- From each fabric, cut 1 strip a **scant** 2″ x full width of fabric for block assembly. Cut the strips in half to make 16 pairs of strips about 20″ long.
- From 3 of the fabrics, cut 12 squares a **scant** 2″ and 12 rectangles a **scant** 2″ x (exactly) 4¾″.
- From the remaining 13 fabrics, cut 16 squares a **scant** 2″ and 16 rectangles a **scant** 2″ x (exactly) 4¾″. (**Note:** Keep sets of matching fabric together. Each set of 4 squares and 4 rectangles will be one block.)
- From the remaining fabric, cut a total of 132 rectangles, a **scant** 2″ × (exactly) 4¾″ for the pieced border.

Light beige

- Cut 61 rectangles a **scant** 2″ × (exactly) 4¾″ for the signature patches.

Beige

- Cut 8 strips a **scant** 2″ × full width of fabric. Cut strips in half to make 16 strips about 20″ long.
- Cut 122 squares 1⅞″. Cut each in half diagonally once to make 244 triangles (A).
- Cut 183 squares 3¼″. Cut each in half diagonally twice to make 732 triangles (B).
- Cut 2 squares 4¼″. Cut each in half diagonally twice to make 8 triangles (C).
- Cut 65 squares 3⅜″. Cut each in half diagonally twice to make 260 triangles (D).
- Cut 4 squares a **scant** 2″. Cut each in half diagonally once to make 8 triangles (E).
- Cut 2 squares 6½″. Cut each in half diagonally once to make 4 triangles (F).
- Cut 5 squares 12⅛″. Cut each in half diagonally twice to make 20 triangles (G).

BLOCK ASSEMBLY

1. Using a matching pair of 20″ print strips, sew 1 print strip to each side of a 20″ beige strip. This strip set should measure 4¾″ wide. Cut the strip set into 8 segments a **scant** 2″ wide. Match the segments to the sets of print squares and rectangles, 2 segments to each set.
2. Sew 2 segments from Step 1 to opposite sides of a light beige signature rectangle to complete the central square.

3. Using 1 set of matching print squares and rectangles, sew 2 beige triangles B to opposite sides of a square. Press. Attach 1 beige triangle A. Make 4 identical units.

Make 4.

4. Sew a print rectangle to 1 of the units created in Step 3. Make 4 corner units.

Make 4.

5. Sew 2 corner units to opposite sides of the central square. Press the seams toward the central square.

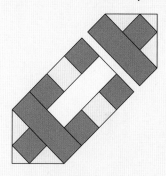

6. Sew 2 beige triangles B to opposite sides of each of the remaining corner units. Make 2. Sew to opposite sides of the block to complete 1 Album block.

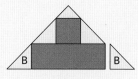

Make 2.

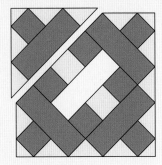

Make 4.

5. Sew a beige triangle D to each end of 60 print rectangles to make 60 mirror-image border units. Sew the mirror-image border units into 4 rows of 15 units.

Make 60.

Make 4.

6. Sew a border center unit between a border unit and a mirror-image border unit. Make 4 pieced borders.

Make 4.

7. Sew 2 beige triangles E to opposite ends of a pieced border, stopping and back-stitching at the seam allowance on the inner corner. Press. Make a second, identical border.

Make 2.

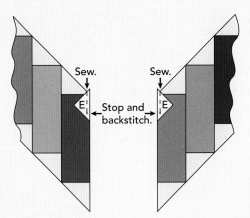

Make 2.

7. Repeat Steps 1–6 to make a total of 61 Album blocks.

QUILT ASSEMBLY

1. Arrange and sew the Album blocks and beige triangles F and G into diagonal rows, following the quilt assembly diagram on page 13. Press.

2. Sew the rows together, pressing after each addition. The quilt should measure 68″ square at this point.

3. Sew 2 C triangles to adjacent sides of a 2⅝″ print square. Sew a print rectangle and then a beige triangle D to each unit. Make 4 border center units.

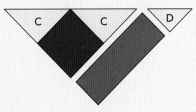

Make 4.

4. Sew a beige triangle D to each end of 64 print rectangles to make 64 border units. Sew the border units into 4 rows of 16 units.

Make 64.

8. Sew the borders created in Step 7 to the sides of the quilt. (**Note:** *The D and E triangles are slightly oversized to make the pieced border fit the quilt. When the borders are sewn to the quilt, the seamline should be slightly beyond the point where the seams cross.*)

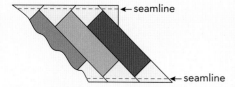

9. Sew 1 beige triangle D and 1 beige triangle E to opposite ends of a print rectangle. Make 2 end units.

Make 2.

10. Sew 1 beige triangle D and 1 beige triangle E to opposite ends of a print rectangle. Make 2 mirror-image end units.

Make 2.

11. Sew 1 end unit and 1 mirror-image end unit to the ends of each remaining pieced border.

Add end unit and mirror-image end unit.

12. Referring to Y-Seam Construction, page 88, sew the borders to the top and bottom of the quilt.

13. Referring to Quilting 101, page 88, layer the quilt top, batting, and backing. Baste. Quilt as desired. Attach a hanging sleeve, if desired, and bind with beige fabric.

Quilt assembly diagram

AUTHORS WHO CONTRIBUTED SIGNATURES TO THE QUILT

Alex Anderson	Monica Ferris	Audrey Niffenegger
Jerry Apps	Earlene Fowler	Brenda Papadakis
Dean Bakopoulos	Linda Franz	Tom Perrotta
Dave Barry	Margaret George	Diane Phalen
Max Barry	Karin Gillespie	Anna Quindlen
Carrie Bebris	Sue Grafton	Lucinda Rosenfeld
Elizabeth Berg	Jane Hamilton	Terry Ryan
Jinny Beyer	M'Liss Rae Hawley	Ami Simms
Judy Blume	Jane Heller	Curtis Sittenfeld
Barbara Brackman	Kevin Henkes	Heather Skyler
Ray Bradbury	Virginia Holman	Charles Slack
Jan Brett	Maddy Hunter	Nicholas Sparks
Eric Carle	Sophie Kinsella	Helen Squire
Jennifer Chiaverini	Lorna Landvik	Timothy Tyson
Beverly Cleary	Chang-rae Lee	Susan Vreeland
Jennifer Crusie	Ursula K. Le Guin	Kate Walbert
Sandra Dallas	John Lescroart	Ayelet Waldman
Tenaya Darlington	Lois Lowry	Jennifer Weiner
Diane Mott Davidson	Jo-Ann Mapson	Rebecca Wells
Mimi Dietrich	Judy Martin	
Lois Duncan	Jacquelyn Mitchard	

Constance's Marriage Quilt

From *The Sugar Camp Quilt* by Jennifer Chiaverini

FINISHED SIZE: 54″ × 66″
FINISHED BLOCK SIZE: 12″ × 12″
NUMBER OF BLOCKS: 12, plus 4 partial blocks for the border
Machine pieced by Jennifer Chiaverini, machine quilted by Sue Vollbrecht, 2006.

FABRIC REQUIREMENTS

- **Green floral:** 1½ yards (includes inner border and binding)
- **Green tone-on-tone:** ½ yard
- **Yellow floral:** ½ yard
- **Yellow tone-on-tone:** ½ yard
- **Blue floral:** ½ yard
- **Blue tone-on-tone:** ½ yard
- **Peach floral:** ½ yard
- **Peach tone-on-tone:** ½ yard
- **Lavender floral:** ½ yard
- **Lavender tone-on-tone:** ½ yard
- **Light cream tone-on-tone:** 2¾ yards
- **Batting:** 58″ × 70″
- **Backing:** 3½ yards

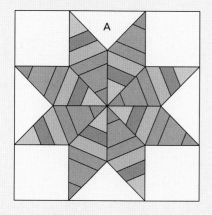

CUTTING

Make templates B and C from the patterns on page 17.

Green floral, green tone-on-tone, yellow floral, yellow tone-on-tone, blue floral, blue tone-on-tone, peach floral, peach tone-on-tone, lavender floral, and lavender tone-on-tone:

- For the blocks, cut the following across the width of **each** of the 10 fabrics:
  - 1 strip 1¼″
  - 1 strip 1½″
  - 1 strip 1¾″
  - 1 strip 2″
  - 1 strip 2¼″
  - 1 strip 2½″

Green floral
- Cut 5 strips 3½″ from the width of fabric for inner border.

Light cream tone-on-tone
- Cut 60 squares 4″.
- Cut 12 squares 6¼″. Cut each in half diagonally twice to make 48 triangles (A).
- Cut 12 squares 3⅜″. Cut each in half diagonally once to make 24 triangles (D) for pieced border.
- Cut 5 strips 6½″ from the width of fabric for outer border.

BLOCK ASSEMBLY

1. Sew the fabric strips together, randomly varying the colors, prints, and widths to make a strip set at least 20″ wide. Press the seams well. Make 4 strip sets.
2. Working from the wrong side of a strip set, position and trace around templates to mark 3 sets of 8 identical diamonds B and 2 sets of 6 identical half-diamonds C, as shown below. Notice that the center line of diamond B lies on the **same** seam for each set of diamonds. Cut out the diamonds and half-diamonds on the marked lines. Repeat for the other 3 strip sets to make a total of 12 sets of 8 diamonds B and 8 sets of 6 half-diamonds C.

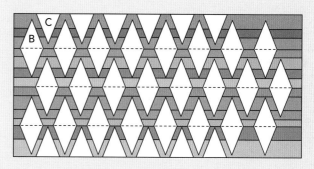

3. Referring to Y-Seam Construction, page 88, mark dots on the wrong side of each diamond B, light cream triangle A, and light cream square.

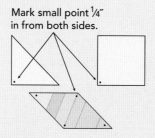

Mark small point ¼″ in from both sides.

4. Arrange the diamonds from one matching set so every other diamond is rotated 180°.

5. Use Y-seam construction to set a light cream triangle A into the angle between 2 adjacent diamonds. Make 4 units.

Make 4.

6. Attach 1 light cream square to the right-hand diamond, taking care not to sew into the seam allowance where the marked point meets the diamond at the widest point, but sewing through the seam allowance at the tip. Make 4 units.

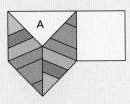

Make 4.

7. Sew together 2 of the units created in Step 6, stitching seams in numerical order in the direction of the arrows. Seam 1 is from the point through the seam allowance on the outer edge. Seam 2 is from point to point. Press. Repeat to make a second identical block half.

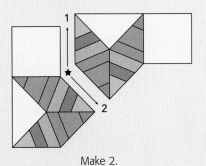

Make 2.

8. Sew the 2 block halves together in the direction of the arrows. Seams 2 and 3 go through the seam allowance on the outer edge.

9. Repeat Steps 3 through 8 with the remaining sets of diamonds to make a total of 12 Star blocks.

QUILT ASSEMBLY

1. Sew the blocks into 4 rows of 3 blocks each. Press.

2. Sew the 4 rows together. Press. The inner quilt should measure 36½″ × 48½″.

3. Sew the green floral inner border strips together diagonally end-to-end and cut 2 strips 42½″ and 2 strips 48½″. Sew the longer strips to the sides of the quilt. Press. Sew the shorter strips to the top and bottom of the quilt. Press. (**Note:** *Always measure your quilt top and adjust the lengths of your borders if necessary.*)

4. Sew the half-diamonds C together along their short sides to make diamonds. Work with 2 sets at a time to make 4 sets of 6 identical diamonds.

5. Arrange the diamonds from one matching set so every other diamond is rotated 180°, as for the block construction.

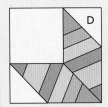

Make 3.

6. Use Y-seam construction to set a light cream square into the angle between 2 adjacent diamonds. Sew 2 small light cream triangles D to opposite sides of each diamond pair. Make 3 star-quarter units.

7. Repeat Steps 5 and 6 to make 3 more sets of identical star-quarter units.

8. From the cream outer-border strips, cut 2 strips 30½″. Sew the remaining strips together diagonally end-to-end and cut 2 strips 42½″.

9. Take 1 star-quarter unit **from each set** and sew to each end of the long outer-border strips.

10. Sew the remaining star-quarter units into matching pairs to make half-stars. Lay out the pieces of all 4 borders to ensure that the identical star points will align when the borders are sewn to the quilt. Sew the half-stars to opposite ends of the short outer-border strips.

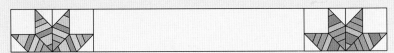

11. Sew the long pieced borders to the sides of the quilt. Press.

12. Sew the short pieced borders to the top and bottom of the quilt. Press.

13. Refer to Quilting 101, page 88 to layer the quilt top, batting, and backing. Baste. Quilt as desired. Attach a hanging sleeve, if desired, and bind with green floral fabric.

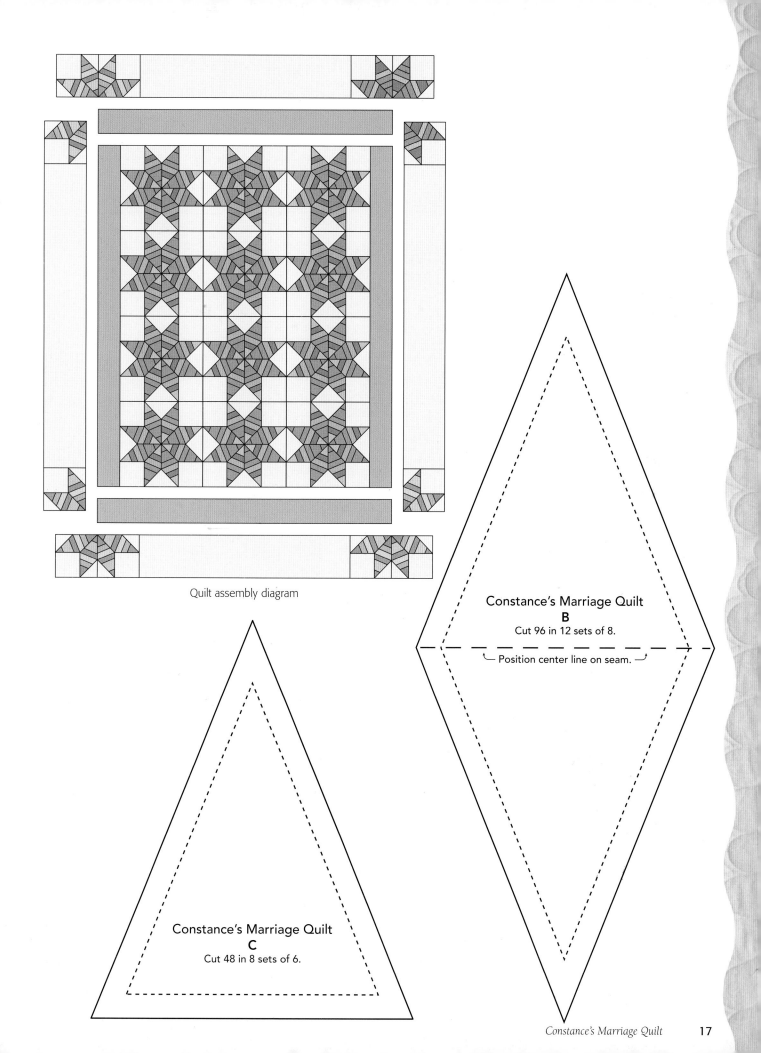

Quilt assembly diagram

Constance's Marriage Quilt
B
Cut 96 in 12 sets of 8.

Position center line on seam.

Constance's Marriage Quilt
C
Cut 48 in 8 sets of 6.

THE SUGAR CAMP QUILT

From *The Sugar Camp Quilt* by Jennifer Chiaverini

FINISHED SIZE: 83¾″ × 83¾″

FINISHED BLOCK SIZE: 10″ × 10″

NUMBER OF BLOCKS: 36 Delectable Mountains blocks, plus 5 landmark blocks for Uncle Jacob's variation

Machine pieced by Jennifer Chiaverini, machine quilted by Sue Vollbrecht, 2005.

FABRIC REQUIREMENTS

- **Dark red:** 1½ yards
- **Blue:** 2⅝ yards (includes border)
- **Brown:** 1 yard
- **Beige:** 3¾ yards
- **Dark blue:** ¾ yard (binding)
- **Batting:** 88″ × 88″
- **Backing:** 7½ yards

For Uncle Jacob's variation:
- **Light red:** ¼ yard
- **Light blue:** ¼ yard
- **Light brown:** ¼ yard

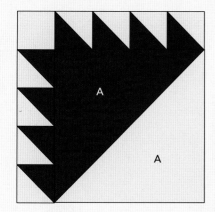

CUTTING

Dark red
- Cut 15 rectangles 6½″ × 9½″.
- Cut 10 squares 8⅞″. Cut each in half diagonally once to make 20 triangles (A).

Blue
- Cut 4 border strips 6½″ × 89″ on the lengthwise grain (parallel to selvage edges).
- Cut 6 rectangles 6½″ × 9½″.
- Cut 4 squares 8⅞″. Cut each in half diagonally once to make 8 triangles (A).

Brown
- Cut 9 rectangles 6½″ × 9½″.
- Cut 6 squares 8⅞″. Cut each in half diagonally once to make 12 triangles (A).

Beige
- Cut 30 rectangles 6½″ × 9½″.
- Cut 16 squares 2½″.
- Cut 18 squares 8⅞″. Cut each in half diagonally once to make 36 triangles (A).
- Cut 3 squares 15½″. Cut each in half diagonally twice to make 12 triangles (B).
- Cut 2 squares 15⅛″. Cut each in half diagonally once to make 4 triangles (C).

BLOCK ASSEMBLY

1. Pair 1 beige rectangle with 1 dark red rectangle, right sides together.
2. Using an accurate photocopier, make 30 copies of the half-square triangle quick-piecing grid on page 22. Securely pin 1 quick-piecing grid to the paired rectangles. (**Note:** *If you prefer, you can reproduce the grid by hand by drawing it on the wrong side of each beige rectangle before pairing it with a dark rectangle.*)
3. Stitching directly through the paper and the fabric, sew on dashed line 1 in the direction of the arrows. Repeat for dashed line 2.
4. Separate the half-square triangle units by cutting on the solid lines. Remove the quick-piecing grid paper. Press the seams toward the darker fabric. The half-square triangle units will measure 2½″ square.
5. Repeat Steps 1–4 for the remaining dark red rectangles and for the blue and brown rectangles to make 172 dark red, 104 brown, and 68 blue half-square triangle units. (**Note:** *This quick-piecing method will result in several extra half-square triangle units.*)
6. Sew 4 dark red half-square triangle units together to make Row 1. Sew 4 additional dark red half-square triangle units to make Row 2, which is a mirror image of Row 1.

Row 1

Row 2

7. Pair 1 dark red triangle A with 1 beige triangle A. Sew them together along the longest edge. Press toward the darker fabric. The pieced square will measure 8½″.
8. Sew Row 1 to the pieced square.
9. Sew 1 beige square to Row 2; then sew this unit to the unit created in Step 8.

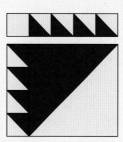

10. Repeat Steps 6–8 to make a total of 16 dark red outer Delectable Mountains blocks.

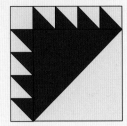

Make 16 dark red outer blocks.

11. Repeat Step 6 using blue and beige triangles A. Repeat Steps 7–9, **except** substitute a brown half-square triangle unit for the beige square in Step 9. Make a total of 8 blue blocks.

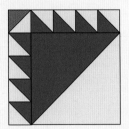

Make 8.

12. Repeat Step 6 using brown and beige triangles A. Repeat Steps 7–9, **except** substitute a dark red half-square triangle unit for the beige square in Step 9. Make a total of 12 brown blocks.

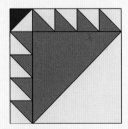

Make 12.

13. Repeat Step 6 to make 4 of Row 1 and 4 of Row 2 with the remaining dark red half-square triangles. Set aside for the Compass Star center block.

COMPASS STAR CENTER BLOCK

Paper-piecing patterns are on pages 22-25.

1. Piece 1 each of foundation paper-piecing patterns D and E. Piece 3 each of foundation paper-piecing patterns F and G. Use light blue and dark blue fabrics for the center stars, light red and dark red fabrics for the outer stars, and beige fabric for the background.

2. Sew D to E to make 1 quarter-block. Sew each F to a G to make 3 quarter-blocks.

3. Sew a DE quarter-block to an FG quarter-block.

4. Sew 2 FG quarter-blocks together.

5. Sew the 2 half-blocks together.

6. Sew a dark red A triangle to each side of the block.

7. Join a Row 1 with a Row 2 to make a half-square triangle strip. Repeat to make 4 half-square triangle strips. Sew 2 strips to opposite sides of the block from Step 3.

8. Sew a blue half-square triangle unit to both ends of the remaining half-square triangle strips. Sew to opposite sides to complete the Compass Star center block.

WORM FENCE

1. From the light brown fabric, cut a strip 1″ × 24″ and sew it into a ¼″ finished tube.

2. Cut the tube as necessary and appliqué it to the quilt, following the quilt assembly diagram for position.

CREEK

Appliqué template pattern is on page 24.

1. Cut 5 H from light blue fabric and prepare them according to your favorite appliqué method.

2. Appliqué the pieces to the quilt top, following the quilt assembly diagram for position.

MILL WHEEL

Make templates I, J, and K from the patterns on page 24.

1. Cut 8 I from beige fabric. Cut 8 J from light brown fabric. Sew each I to a J. Join the units in pairs; then join the pairs to make a block half. Sew the halves together.

2. Cut an octagon K from light brown fabric and prepare it according to your favorite appliqué method. Appliqué it to the center of the block.

3. Appliqué the mill wheel to the quilt top, following the quilt assembly diagram for position.

INDIAN TRAIL

Paper-piecing patterns are on page 25.

1. Piece 2 each of foundation piecing patterns L and N. Piece 1 each of foundation piecing patterns M and O. Use beige, light blue, and light brown fabrics.

2. Sew the units together as shown below.

3. Appliqué the completed unit to the quilt, following the quilt assembly diagram below for position.

QUILT ASSEMBLY

1. Arrange and sew the Delectable Mountains blocks, beige triangles B, and beige triangles C into diagonal rows, following the quilt assembly diagram below. Press.

2. Sew the rows together, pressing after each addition. The inner quilt should measure $71\frac{3}{4}'' \times 71\frac{3}{4}''$.

3. Referring to Mitered Borders, page 90, sew the border strips to the quilt. (**Note:** *Always measure your quilt top and adjust the lengths of your borders if necessary.*)

4. Referring to Quilting 101, page 88, layer the quilt top, batting, and backing. Baste. Quilt as desired. Attach a hanging sleeve, if desired, and bind with dark blue fabric.

Quilt assembly diagram

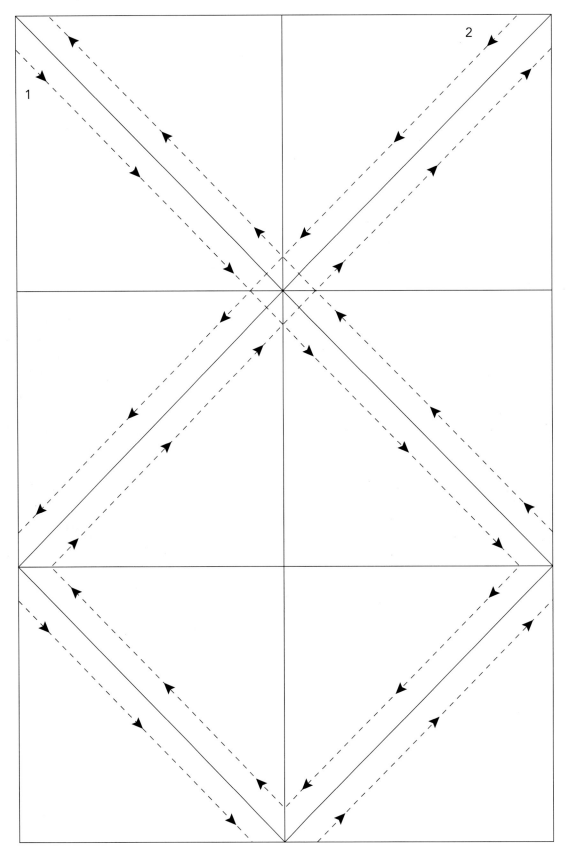

Half-square triangle quick-piecing grid

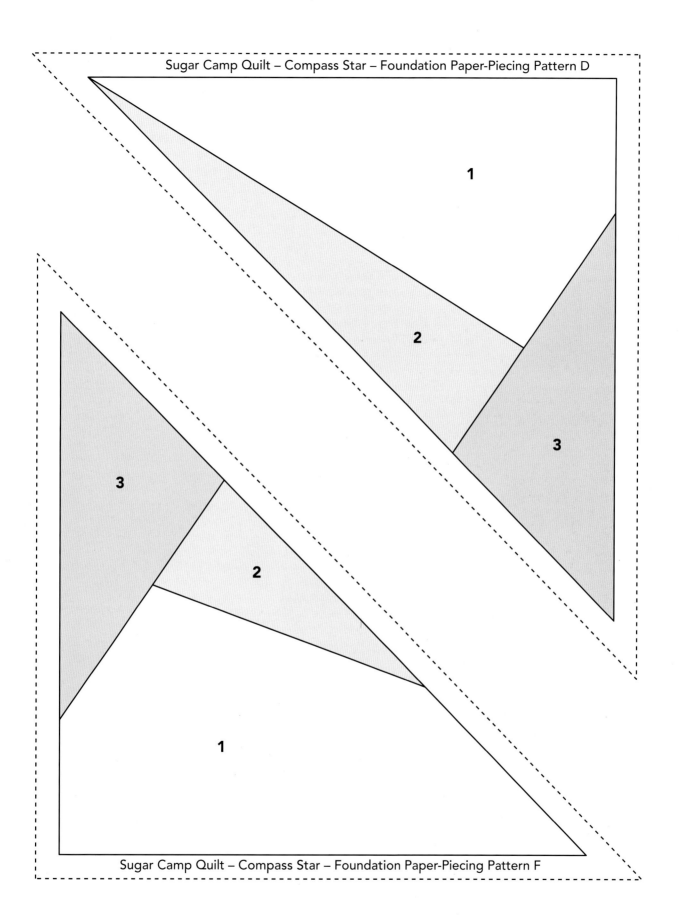

Sugar Camp Quilt – Compass Star – Foundation Paper-Piecing Pattern D

1

2

3

3

2

1

Sugar Camp Quilt – Compass Star – Foundation Paper-Piecing Pattern F

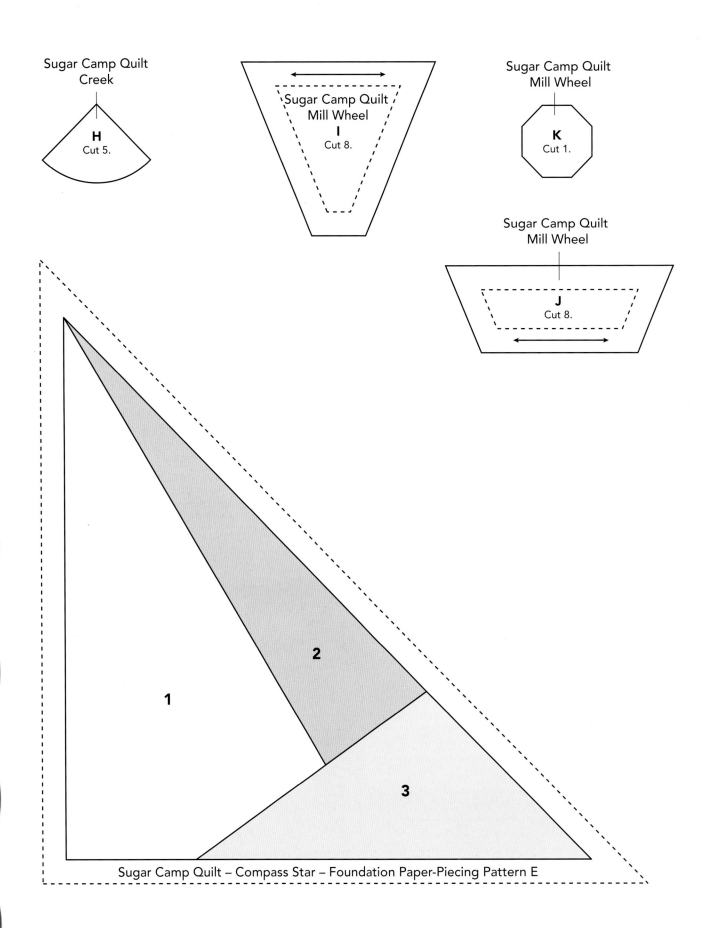

Sugar Camp Quilt
Creek

H
Cut 5.

Sugar Camp Quilt
Mill Wheel
I
Cut 8.

Sugar Camp Quilt
Mill Wheel

K
Cut 1.

Sugar Camp Quilt
Mill Wheel

J
Cut 8.

1

2

3

Sugar Camp Quilt – Compass Star – Foundation Paper-Piecing Pattern E

Sugar Camp Quilt – Indian Trail – Foundation
Paper-Piecing Pattern L

Sugar Camp Quilt – Indian Trail – Foundation
Paper-Piecing Pattern M

Sugar Camp Quilt – Indian Trail – Foundation
Paper-Piecing Pattern N

Sugar Camp Quilt – Indian Trail – Foundation
Paper-Piecing Pattern O

Sugar Camp Quilt – Compass Star – Foundation Paper-Piecing Pattern G

FROM *The Christmas Quilt*

When Christmas Eve comes to Elm Creek Manor, the tenor of the holiday is far from certain. Sylvia Bergstrom Compson has her own reasons for preferring a quiet, even subdued, Christmas. Her young friend Sarah McClure, however, takes the opposite view, and decides to deck the halls brightly. Sarah discovers a curious Christmas quilt packed amongst the trunks of Bergstrom family decorations that haven't been touched in more than fifty years. Begun in seasonal fabrics and patterns, the quilt remains unfinished.

Sylvia reveals that the handiwork spans several generations and a quartet of Bergstrom quilters—her great-aunt, her mother, her sister, and herself. As she examines the array of quilt blocks each family member contributed but never completed, memories of Christmases past emerge.

At Elm Creek Manor, Christmas began as a celebration of simple virtues—joy and hope buoyed by the spirit of giving. As each successive generation of Bergstroms lived through its unique trials—the antebellum era, the Great Depression, World War II—tradition offered sustenance even during the most difficult times. Sylvia's tales at first seem to inform her family legacy, but ultimately illuminate far more, from the importance of women's art to its place in commemorating our shared experience, at Christmastime and in every season.

As longtime *Elm Creek Quilts* readers know, when I wrote *The Quilter's Apprentice*, I had no idea it would become the first of a series. Even *Round Robin*, my second novel, was intended only as a sequel to the first book—and unaware that I might be aging my characters too quickly, I allowed two years to elapse between the first two novels! When it came time to write *The Christmas Quilt*, I set the story within that skipped interval to help fill in those in-between years.

Christmas Memories, pieced and appliquéd by Carol Hattan, is the Christmas quilt of the novel's title, showcasing the beautiful handwork of several generations of Bergstrom women. *Christmas Greetings From Elm Creek Manor*, however, does not appear within the story, but was inspired by the artwork from Honi Werner's beautiful cover and Melanie Parks's lovely endpapers. So many readers wrote to me requesting patterns for these illustrations that I decided to put them together in a medallion-style sampler that perfectly captures the joy and good cheer of the season.

Sylvia Bergstrom Compson

Born into a prosperous family in rural central Pennsylvania, Sylvia loves her family estate, Elm Creek Manor, and plans one day to take her place alongside her father in the family horse-breeding business, Bergstrom Thoroughbreds. Tragedy during World War II and a sister's betrayal drive her from her beloved home and force her to choose a new path. A gifted quilter, Sylvia graduates with a degree in Art Education from Carnegie Mellon University in Pittsburgh. For many years she teaches in the Sewickley, Pennsylvania, area, and she becomes a renowned lecturer at quilt shows and quilt guilds across the country. Upon her return to Elm Creek Manor after a fifty-year absence, Sylvia and her young apprentice, Sarah McClure, turn the manor into Elm Creek Quilt Camp, a retreat for quilters.

Sarah McClure

Sarah McClure, a former cost accountant unsatisfied with her career, is hired to help Sylvia prepare Elm Creek Manor for sale. After quilting lessons become the foundation for a blossoming friendship between the two women, Sarah proposes turning Elm Creek Manor into a retreat for quilters. As successful as Sarah is in business matters, she is less adept at navigating the rocky emotional terrain between herself and her mother. She responds with reluctance whenever Sylvia urges her to learn from her own mistakes and reconcile with her mother before it's too late.

Matt McClure

The McClures move to Waterford, Pennsylvania, after Matt obtains a job as a landscape architect with a local company, a position he leaves after the founding of Elm Creek Quilt Camp to become the estate's caretaker. For the most part Matt enjoys his new role, especially tending to the manor's orchards and gardens, but he sometimes worries that the McClures' future is precariously balanced on the success or failure of the fledgling quilt camp. Like Sylvia, he wishes that Sarah had a better relationship with her mother, and is willing to ignore his mother-in-law's slights against him for the sake of family harmony.

Claudia Bergstrom Midden

The eldest child of Frederick and Eleanor Bergstrom, Claudia is born in 1918 while her father is serving overseas in World War I. After Claudia nearly dies in the influenza pandemic, her mother becomes especially protective of her, which young Sylvia interprets as favoritism. Sylvia's misguided jealousy, coupled with Claudia's bossiness and vanity, yields intense sisterly friction. Unbeknownst to Sylvia, Claudia's outward confidence and air of superiority mask deep-seated insecurities, for she is painfully aware that she does not possess her younger sister's creative gifts. Claudia's seams rarely match and she often cuts off triangle tips, errors that make her quilts easily identifiable to Sylvia.

Eleanor Lockwood Bergstrom

The younger of two daughters born to a wealthy department store magnate, Eleanor suffered from poor health as a child and was not expected to survive into adulthood. Virtually ignored by her distant and self-absorbed parents, Eleanor is raised by her nanny, an independent and radical woman who teaches Eleanor to think for herself rather than blindly follow convention. When her elder sister elopes with her father's business rival, Eleanor is expected to secure her family's waning fortunes by marrying her sister's jilted fiancé, but she defies her parents by marrying Frederick Bergstrom for love. Though estranged from her parents, Eleanor never regrets her decision, and eventually becomes the mother of three children, including Sylvia.

Lucinda Bergstrom

Sylvia's great-aunt is the youngest daughter of Hans and Anneke Bergstrom, founders of Elm Creek Farm and the first members of the family to come to the United States from Germany. An accomplished quilter and baker, Lucinda is the caretaker of family history and entrances young Sylvia with her stories of the manor's earliest years, although she does not share all of her secrets. Lucinda never marries, a fact that is of no concern to Sylvia as a child but piques her curiosity in later years.

*S*ylvia sank to her knees beside the box, overwhelmed by the sensation of discovery and loss. She had never forgotten the Christmas quilt, nor had she ever expected to see it again. Begun by her Great-Aunt Lucinda when Sylvia was very young, the unfinished quilt had been taken up and worked upon by a succession of Bergstrom women—among them, Sylvia herself. From what she could see of the folded bundle of patchwork and appliqué, not a single stitch had been added since she last worked upon it. And yet every intricate Feathered Star block, every graceful appliquéd cluster of holly leaves and berries had been tucked away as neatly as if a conscientious quiltmaker had had every intention of completing her masterpiece. Even the scraps of fabric had been sorted according to color—greens here, reds there, golds and creams in their own separate piles. The Christmas quilt had been abandoned, but it had not been discarded.

—Excerpted from *The Christmas Quilt* by Jennifer Chiaverini

*S*ylvia sat pondering while Sarah worked on the Christmas quilt, ruefully aware that her plan to bring together Sarah and her mother had been doomed from the beginning. Their relationship was clearly in worse shape than Sylvia had realized, and no thrown-together Christmas reunion would rectify things. Christmas was the season of peace, but somehow people often forgot to include the harmony of their own family in their prayers for peace on earth and goodwill toward all… No wonder Sarah preferred to work on another family's abandoned quilt than on her own family's unresolved disagreements.

Sarah did seem to be making remarkable progress on the quilt… She had attached border sashing to some of Lucinda's Feathered Stars and joined four together in pairs. With a few added seams, Eleanor's holly sprays had been transformed into open plumes, which Sarah was in the midst of attaching to Claudia's Variable Stars.

"That's a sure way to ruin it," muttered Sylvia. Louder, over the cheerful clatter of the sewing machine, she added, "Sarah, dear, I thought I told you not to bother including Claudia's blocks in the quilt."

Amused, Sarah said, "You suggested that I could leave them out if I thought they would ruin the quilt, and I told you that I wouldn't dream of leaving her out of a family quilt. I measured, and you're right; her blocks vary in size almost a half-inch, but my layout will account for that."

"But they're so plain and simple," protested Sylvia. "They aren't as intricate as the blocks my mother and great-aunt made."

"That's precisely why they work so well." Sarah continued sewing, completely indifferent to Sylvia's consternation. "Sometimes a simple block is needed to set off more elaborate designs. You taught me that."

Sylvia had always suspected that someday her preaching would come back to haunt her.

—Excerpted from *The Christmas Quilt* by Jennifer Chiaverini

CHRISTMAS MEMORIES

From *The Christmas Quilt* by Jennifer Chiaverini

FINISHED SIZE: 84″ × 112″
FINISHED BLOCK SIZE: 18″ × 18″ Feathered Stars and Holly Wreaths, 8″ × 8″ Variable Stars, 7″ × 7″ Log Cabins
NUMBER OF BLOCKS: 6 Feathered Stars, 5 Variable Stars, 2 Holly Wreaths, 4 Holly Swags, 52 Log Cabins
Machine pieced, hand appliquéd, and hand quilted by Carol Hattan, 2005.

FABRIC REQUIREMENTS

- **White**: 7 ¾ yards (includes sashing and inner border)
- **Red**: 1 yard
- **Dark greens**: 3½ yards (includes binding)
- **Medium greens**: 2 yards
- **Light neutrals**: 1½ yards (for Log Cabin border)
- **Batting**: 88″ × 116″
- **Backing**: 9¾ yards

SASHING AND INNER BORDERS

CUTTING

Cut all sashing and inner border strips on the lengthwise grain (parallel to selvage edges).

White

- Cut 2 strips 5½″ × 98½″ for side inner borders.
- Cut 2 strips 6½″ × 60½″ for top and bottom inner borders.
- Cut 2 strips 3½″ × 86½″ for vertical sashing.
- Cut 6 rectangles 3½″ × 18½″ for horizontal sashing.
- Cut 2 rectangles 8½″ × 18½″ for horizontal sashing.

FEATHERED STARS

CUTTING

Make templates A, B, and C from the patterns on page 33.

White

- Cut 120 squares 2⅛″ (D).
- Cut 24 squares 2⅜″. Cut each in half diagonally once to make 48 triangles (E).
- Cut 48 squares 2⅛″. Cut each in half diagonally once to make 96 triangles (F).
- Cut 24 squares 5¾″ (G).
- Cut 6 squares 8¾″. Cut each in half diagonally twice to make 24 triangles (H).

Red

- Cut 6 octagons (B).
- Cut 48 diamonds (A).

Dark and medium greens

- Cut 48 kites (C) in sets of 8 per block, using the medium greens for 2 or 3 blocks.

Dark greens

- Cut 120 squares 2⅛″ (D).

BLOCK ASSEMBLY

1. Sew 4 triangles E to 4 opposite sides of octagon B.

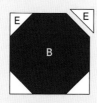

2. Referring to Half-Square Triangle Blocks, page 88, make 40 quick-pieced half-square triangle units using the dark green and white squares D. Trim the finished half-square triangle units to a scant 1¾″ square.

3. Sew together 3 half-square triangle units and 1 white triangle F to make a Feather strip 1. Make 8. Sew together 2 half-square triangle units and 1 white triangle F to make a Feather strip 2. Make 8.

Feather strip 1. Make 8.

Feather strip 2. Make 8.

4. Sew a red diamond A to the triangle tip of 4 Feather strips 1 and 4 Feather strips 2. (**Note**: *Set aside the strips without red diamonds until the next step.*) Sew a Feather strip 2/A unit to each white square G. Add a Feather strip 1/A unit. Make 4 corner units.

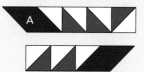

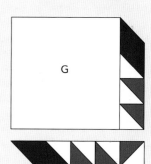

Corner unit; Make 4.

5. Sewing only to the middle of white triangle F, attach a Feather strip 2 to each large white triangle H. In the same manner, attach a Feather strip 1.

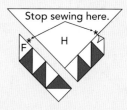

6. Sew a green kite C to each of the units created in Step 5. Sew 1 white triangle E to each remaining C and attach to each unit to complete 4 side units.

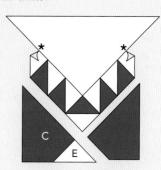

Side unit; Make 4.

7. Sew 2 side units to opposite sides of the octagon unit to make the center row.

8. Sew 2 corner units to opposite sides of each remaining side unit. Complete the unfinished partial seam by sewing white triangles H to the feather strips and diamonds.

9. Sew the top, center, and bottom rows together. Complete the unfinished partial seams.

10. Repeat Steps 1–9 to make 6 Feathered Stars.

VARIABLE STARS

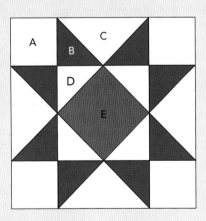

CUTTING

White

- Cut 20 squares 2½″ (A).
- Cut 5 squares 5¼″. Cut each in half diagonally twice to yield 20 triangles (C).
- Cut 10 squares 2⅞″. Cut each in half diagonally once to yield 20 triangles (D).

- Cut 10 rectangles 5½″ × 8½″.
- Cut 8 rectangles 5½″ × 18½″.

Red

- Cut 5 squares 4⅝″ (E).

Dark green

- Cut 20 squares 2⅞″. Cut each in half diagonally once to make 40 triangles (B).

BLOCK ASSEMBLY

1. Sew a dark green triangle B to each side of a white triangle C to make a Flying Geese unit. Press. Make 20.

Make 20.

2. Sew a triangle D to 2 opposite sides of a red square E. Press. Sew a triangle D to the other 2 sides of the square to make a square-in-a-square unit. Press. Make 5.

3. Sew 4 white squares A, 4 Flying Geese units, and 1 square-in-a-square unit in rows to make a Variable Star block. Make 5.

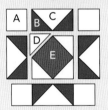

Make 5.

4. Sew a white 5½″ × 8½″ rectangle to opposite sides of each Variable Star block. Set aside 1 of these units to be the quilt center.

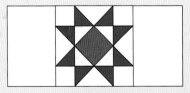

5. Sew a white 5½″ × 18½″ rectangle to the top and bottom of the 4 remaining Variable Star blocks.

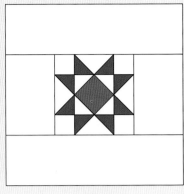

Make 4.

HOLLY WREATHS

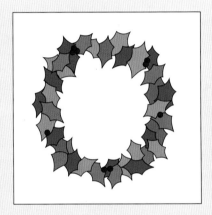

CUTTING

Appliqué template patterns are on page 34.

White

- Cut 2 squares 19½″.

Red

- Cut 18 berries (D) and prepare them according to your favorite appliqué method.

Dark and medium greens

- Cut a total of 68 leaves (A, B, and C) in a mixture of sizes and prepare them according to your favorite appliqué method.

BLOCK ASSEMBLY

1. With a pencil, lightly draw an 11″ circle in the center of a white square. Appliqué half of the leaves in a random arrangement to cover the pencil line. Appliqué berries D on top, following the block diagram for position.

2. Centering the design, trim the block to 18½″ square (includes seam allowance). Make 2 Holly Wreath blocks.

QUILT ASSEMBLY

1. Sew the blocks together in 3 vertical rows, inserting the white 3½ × 18½″ and 8½″ × 18½″ sashing strips, as shown in the quilt assembly diagram on page 32. Press.

2. Sew the 3 rows together with a white 3½″ × 86½″ sashing strip between each pair of rows. Press.

3. Add the white 6½″ × 60½″ top and bottom inner borders. Press.

4. Add the white 5½″ × 98½″ side borders. Press.

HOLLY SWAGS

The holly swags should be appliquéd after the inner quilt top is constructed because they overlap the white inner borders.

CUTTING

Appliqué template patterns are on page 34.

Red
- Cut 48 berries (D) and prepare them according to your favorite appliqué method.

Dark green
- Cut a total of 80 leaves (A, B, and C) in a mixture of sizes and prepare them according to your favorite appliqué method.

- Cut 4 bias strips 1⅛″ × 22″ for stems.

ASSEMBLY

1. Fold a bias strip in half lengthwise, wrong sides together, and press lightly. Pin the strip to the quilt in an arc, as shown in the quilt assembly diagram on page 32.

2. Sew the bias strip to the quilt ¼″ from the raw edges. Fold the pressed edge over the stitching and sew along the fold using hand or machine appliqué.

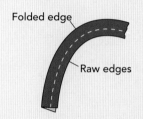

Sew ¼″ from the raw edges of the strip.

3. Repeat Steps 1 and 2 on each corner of the quilt.

4. Appliqué the holly leaves and berries along each bias strip. Cover the raw ends of the bias strips with holly leaves.

LOG CABIN BORDER

CUTTING

Red
- Cut 52 squares 1½″ (A).

Dark and medium greens
- Cut 4 squares 1½″ (B).
- Cut 56 rectangles 1½″ × 2½″ (C and D).
- Cut 56 rectangles 1½″ × 3½″ (E and F).
- Cut 56 rectangles 1½″ × 4½″ (G and H).
- Cut 56 rectangles 1½″ × 5½″ (I and J).
- Cut 56 rectangles 1½″ × 6½″ (K and L).
- Cut 52 rectangles 1½″ × 7½″ (M).

Light neutrals
- Cut 48 squares 1½″ (B).
- Cut 48 rectangles 1½″ × 2½″ (C).

- Cut 48 rectangles 1½″ × 3½″ (F).
- Cut 48 rectangles 1½″ × 4½″ (G).
- Cut 48 rectangles 1½″ × 5½″ (J).
- Cut 48 rectangles 1½″ × 6½″ (K).

ASSEMBLY

1. Sew a red center square A to a neutral square B. Add neutral and green rectangles in order from shortest to longest. Make 48 neutral/green Log Cabin blocks.

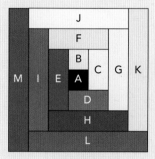

Make 48.

2. Sew a red center square A to a green square B. Add green rectangles in order from shortest to longest. Make 4 all-green Log Cabin blocks for the quilt corners.

Make 4.

3. Make a strip of 10 neutral/green Log Cabin blocks, as shown in the quilt assembly diagram on page 32. Make 2. Sew the strips to the top and bottom of the quilt. Press.

4. Make a strip of 14 neutral/green Log Cabin blocks, as shown in the quilt assembly diagram on page 32. Add 1 all-green Log Cabin block to the end of each strip. Make 2. Sew the side Log Cabin borders to the quilt. Press.

5. Referring to Quilting 101, page 88, layer the quilt top, batting, and backing. Baste. Quilt as desired. Attach a hanging sleeve, if desired, and bind with dark green fabric.

Quilt assembly diagram

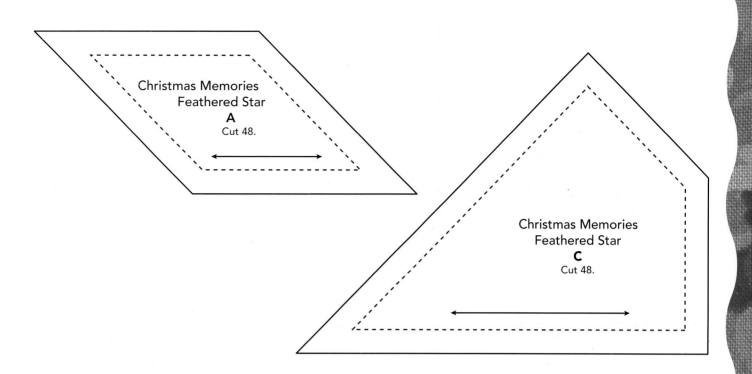

Christmas Memories
Feathered Star
A
Cut 48.

Christmas Memories
Feathered Star
C
Cut 48.

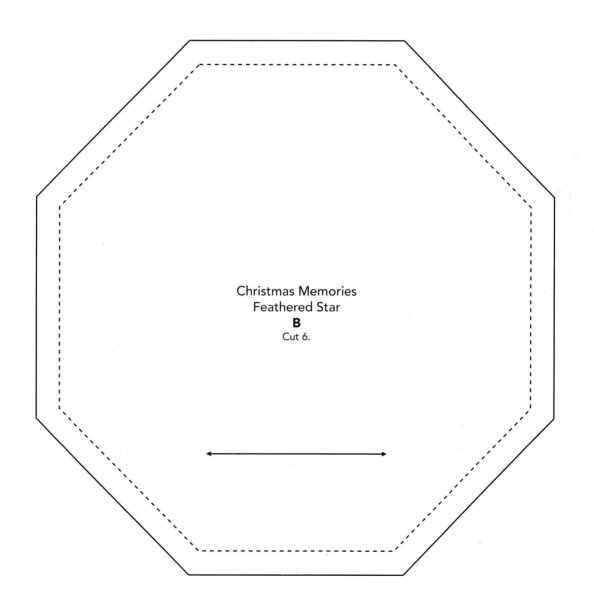

Christmas Memories
Feathered Star
B
Cut 6.

Christmas Memories
Holly Wreath and Swag
A
Cut 49.

Christmas Memories
Holly Wreath and Swag
B
Cut 49.

Christmas Memories
Holly Wreath and Swag
C
Cut 50.

Christmas Memories
Holly Wreath and Swag
Cut 66.

D

CHRISTMAS GREETINGS
From Elm Creek Manor

From *The Christmas Quilt* by Jennifer Chiaverini

FINISHED SIZE: 64″ × 64″
FINISHED BLOCK SIZE: 12″ × 12″; center, 24″ × 24″
NUMBER OF BLOCKS: 12, plus 1 center block
Machine pieced and appliquéd by Jennifer Chiaverini, machine quilted by Sue Vollbrecht, 2006.
The Elm Creek Quilts: *The Christmas Quilt Collection* fabrics used in this quilt were generously donated
by Red Rooster Fabrics. The center appliqué portrait was inspired by the cover art of Honi Werner.

FABRIC REQUIREMENTS

- **Golden beige:** 5 yards
- **Dark green:** 2½ yards
- **Medium green:** 1½ yards
- **Light green:** 1 yard
- **Dark red:** 3½ yards (includes binding)
- **Gold:** 1 yard
- **Light blue:** 1 yard
- **White:** 1 yard
- **Batting:** 68″ × 68″
- **Backing:** 4 yards

CHRISTMAS CACTUS

CUTTING

Appliqué template patterns are on page 45.

Golden beige
- Cut 1 square 14″.

Dark green
- Cut 1 square 12″.

Dark red
- Cut 24 buds (B) and prepare them according to your favorite appliqué method.
- Cut 4 buds (C) and prepare them according to your favorite appliqué method.

BLOCK ASSEMBLY

1. Fold the golden beige square in half horizontally, vertically, and twice diagonally, pressing after each fold to mark the square's center and to create placement marks.

2. Cut a 14″ square from freezer paper. Fold it into quarters. Trace template pattern A onto the freezer paper, aligning the dashed lines with the folds. Cut out the traced design, paper-snowflake fashion, to make the freezer paper template.

3. Using a lightbox or sunny window, lightly mark the placement of the appliqué shapes on the golden beige square, ⅛″ inside the pattern lines.

4. Using the freezer paper template and the dark green square, prepare 1 cactus appliqué A using your favorite appliqué method.

5. Appliqué the dark green cactus A to the golden beige square. Appliqué the red buds B and C in place.

6. Centering the design, trim the block to 12½″ square (includes seam allowance).

STAR OF THE MAGI

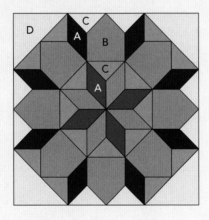

CUTTING

Make templates A and B from the patterns on pages 45–46.

Golden beige
- Cut 2 squares 3¾″. Cut each in half diagonally twice to make 8 triangles (C).
- Cut 2 squares 4⅜″. Cut each in half diagonally once to make 4 triangles (D).

Dark green
- Cut 4 diamonds (A).

Medium green
- Cut 4 diamonds (A).
- Cut 8 pentagons (B).

Dark red
- Cut 8 diamonds (A).

Gold
- Cut 4 squares 3¾″. Cut each in half diagonally twice to make 16 triangles (C).

BLOCK ASSEMBLY

1. Referring to Y-Seam Construction, page 88, mark dots on the wrong side of each diamond A, pentagon B, and triangle C.

2. Use Y-seam construction to set a gold triangle C into the angle between a medium green diamond A and a dark green triangle diamond A. Sewing from point to point only, attach another gold triangle C to the medium green diamond A. Make 4.

Make 4.

3. Using Y-seam construction, join the units created in Step 2 into pairs and sew them together to complete the central octagon.

4. Sewing from point to point only, sew 2 dark red diamonds A to opposite sides of a medium green pentagon B. Using Y-seam construction, attach 2 gold triangles C. Make 4 corner units.

Make 4.

5. Sew 4 medium green pentagons B to opposite sides of the central octagon. Using Y-seam construction, attach the corner units to the central octagon.

6. Using Y-seam construction, set small golden beige triangles C into the angles between pentagons B and red diamonds A.

7. Attach the large golden beige triangles D to the corners to complete the block.

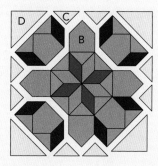

STAR OF BETHLEHEM

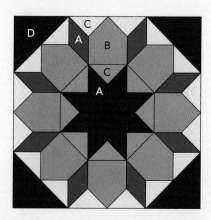

CUTTING

Make templates A and B from the patterns on pages 45–46.

Golden beige

- Cut 4 squares 3¾″. Cut each in half diagonally twice to make 16 triangles (C).

Dark green

- Cut 8 diamonds (A).

Medium green

- Cut 8 pentagons (B).

Dark red

- Cut 8 diamonds (A).
- Cut 2 squares 4⅜″. Cut each in half diagonally once to make 4 triangles (D).

Gold

- Cut 2 squares 3¾″. Cut each in half diagonally twice to make 8 triangles (C).

BLOCK ASSEMBLY

Follow the directions for making the Star of the Magi block, page 36, following the block diagram for color placement.

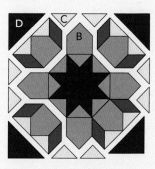

ADVENT WREATH

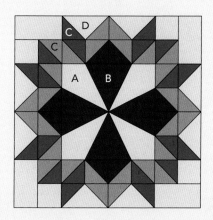

CUTTING

Make templates A and B from the patterns on page 47.

Golden beige

- Cut 4 kites (A).
- Cut 4 rectangles 2″ × 3½″.
- Cut 4 squares 2″.
- Cut 2 squares 4¼″. Cut each in half diagonally twice to make 8 background triangles (D).

Dark green

- Cut 12 squares 2⅜″. Cut 4 of the squares in half diagonally once to make 8 triangles (C). Set the other 8 squares aside.

Medium green

- Cut 12 squares 2⅜″. Cut 4 of the squares in half diagonally once to make 8 triangles (C). Set the other 8 squares aside.

Dark red

- Cut 4 triangles (B).
- Cut 4 squares 2⅜″.

BLOCK ASSEMBLY

1. Sew each golden beige kite A to a dark red triangle B. Join these units into pairs and sew them together to make the central square.

2. Sew a medium green triangle C and a dark green triangle C to opposite sides of a triangle D. Make 8 identical Flying Geese units. Sew the units into pairs.

Make 4.

3. Pair 6 medium green squares with 6 dark green squares, right sides together. Referring to Half-Square Triangle Blocks, page 88, make 12 medium green/dark green half-square triangle units. Pair each remaining medium green square with a dark red square and use the same method to make 8 dark red/medium green half-square triangle units.

4. Sew together 4 half-square triangle units into a row. Make 4 identical rows.

Make 4.

5. Sew each row of half-square triangle units to a Flying Geese pair.

6. Sew 2 of the units created in Step 5 to opposite sides of the central square.

7. Sew 1 remaining medium green/ dark green half-square triangle unit to a golden beige square. Sew a golden beige rectangle to each unit to make a corner unit. Make 4 corner units.

Make 4.

8. Sew the units together to complete the block. Press.

CHRISTMAS EVE

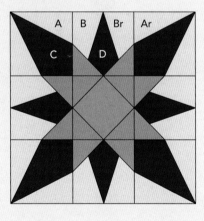

CUTTING

Make templates A, B, C, and D from the patterns on pages 46–47.

Golden beige

- Cut 4 triangles (A). Flip the template over and cut 4 Ar.
- Cut 4 trapezoids (B). Flip the template over and cut 4 Br.

Medium green

- Cut 6 squares $2\frac{7}{8}''$. Cut each in half diagonally once to make 12 triangles.

Dark red

- Cut 4 kites (C).
- Cut 4 kites (D).

Gold

- Cut 1 square $3\frac{3}{8}''$.

BLOCK ASSEMBLY

1. Sew 4 medium green triangles to the gold square.

2. Sew 1 A and 1 Ar to each C.

3. Sew 1 B and 1 Br to each D. Sew 2 medium green triangles to each unit.

4. Sew the units into 3 rows. Sew the rows together.

CHRISTMAS STAR

CUTTING

Make template A from the pattern on page 46.

Golden beige

- Cut 1 square $4\frac{1}{2}''$ (B).
- Cut 8 squares $2\frac{1}{2}''$ (C).
- Cut 2 squares $5\frac{1}{4}''$. Cut each in half diagonally twice to make 8 large triangles (D).
- Cut 2 squares $3\frac{1}{4}''$. Cut each in half diagonally twice to make 8 small triangles (E).

Dark green

- Cut 8 squares $2\frac{7}{8}''$. Cut each in half diagonally once to make 16 triangles (F).

Dark red

- Cut 4 squares (A).
- Cut 1 square $5\frac{1}{4}''$. Cut the square in half diagonally twice to make 4 triangles (D).

BLOCK ASSEMBLY

1. Sew 2 small triangles E to a dark red square. Sew 2 dark green triangles F to each unit. Make 4.

Make 4.

2. Sew 2 units to opposite sides of the large square B.

3. Sew 1 small golden beige square C to each end of the remaining 2 units.

Make 2.

4. Sew the units from Step 3 to opposites sides of the center unit to create the central star.

5. Sew 2 golden beige triangles D to a dark red triangle D. Sew 2 green triangles F to opposite sides of this unit to complete a side unit. Make 4 side units.

Make 4.

6. Sew side units to opposite sides of the central star.

7. Sew 2 golden beige squares C to opposite ends of each remaining side unit.

8. Sew the 3 rows together. Press.

FLOWER OF CHRISTMAS

CUTTING

Appliqué template pattern is on page 47.

Golden beige

- Cut 1 square 6½" (A).
- Cut 4 rectangles 2¼" × 4".
- Cut 4 squares 2¼" (C).
- Cut 3 squares 3¾". Cut each in half diagonally twice to make 12 triangles.

Dark green

- Cut 1 strip 1¾" × 40".

Dark red

- Cut 1 strip 1¾" × 20".
- Cut 4 leaves (F) and prepare them according to your favorite appliqué method.

BLOCK ASSEMBLY

1. Trim one end of the dark green strip at a 45° angle. Align a ruler with the cut edge and cut 16 diamonds 2¼" wide. Referring to Y-Seam Construction, page 88, mark dots on the wrong side of each diamond, golden beige triangle, and rectangle B.

2. Using the method described in Step 1, cut and mark 8 diamonds from the dark red strip.

3. Sew 2 red diamonds to the short sides of a golden beige triangle. Make 4. Sew these units to opposite sides of golden beige square A.

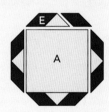

4. Use Y-seam construction to set a golden beige triangle into the angle between 2 green diamonds. Make 8 star-point units.

5. Sew a golden beige square C to a star-point unit. Use Y-seam construction to sew this unit to another star-point unit. Make 4 corner units.

Make 4.

6. Sewing from point to point only, attach the golden beige rectangles B to opposite sides of the central unit.

7. Using Y-seam construction, sew the corner units to the block.

8. Appliqué the 4 dark red leaves F to the center of the block.

FEATHERED STAR

CUTTING

Make templates A, B, and C from the patterns on page 49.

Golden beige

- Cut 20 squares 1⅝" (D).
- Cut 4 squares 1⅞". Cut each in half diagonally once to make 8 triangles (E).
- Cut 8 squares 1⅝". Cut each in half diagonally once to make 16 triangles (F).
- Cut 4 squares 4" (G).
- Cut 1 square 6¼". Cut the square in half diagonally twice to make 4 triangles (H).

Dark green

- Cut 8 kites (C).
- Cut 20 squares 1⅝" (D).

Dark red

- Cut 8 diamonds (A).
- Cut 1 octagon (B).

BLOCK ASSEMBLY

1. Sew 4 small triangles E to 4 opposite sides of octagon B.

2. Referring to Half-Square Triangle Blocks, page 88, make 40 quick-pieced half-square triangle units using the dark green and golden beige squares D.

3. Sew together 3 half-square triangle units and 1 golden beige triangle F to make a Feather strip 1. Make 8. Sew 2 half-square triangle units and 1 golden beige triangle F to make a Feather strip 2. Make 8.

Feather strip 1. Make 8.   Feather strip 2. Make 8.

4. Sew a red diamond A to the triangle tip of 4 Feather strips 1 and 4 Feather strips 2. (*Note: Set aside the strips without red diamonds until the next step.*) Sew a Feather strip 2/A unit to each golden beige square G. Add a Feather strip 1/A unit. Make 4 corner units.

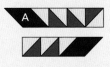

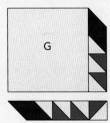

Corner unit; Make 4.

5. Sewing only to the middle of triangle F, attach a Feather strip 2 to each large golden beige triangle H. In the same manner, attach a Feather strip 1.

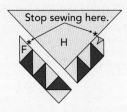

6. Sew a green kite C to each of the units created in Step 5. Sew 1 golden beige triangle E to each remaining kite and attach to complete the side units. Make 4.

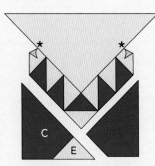

Side unit; Make 4.

7. Sew 2 side units to opposite sides of the octagon unit to make the center row.

8. Sew 2 corner units to opposite sides of each remaining side unit. Complete the unfinished partial seam by sewing the golden beige triangle to the feather strips and diamonds.

9. Sew the top, center, and bottom rows together. Complete the unfinished partial seams.

MANGER

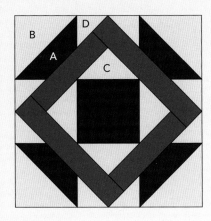

CUTTING

Make template A from the pattern on page 48.

Golden beige

- Cut 2 squares $4\frac{7}{8}''$. Cut each in half diagonally once to make 4 triangles (B).
- Cut 2 squares $3\frac{3}{4}''$. Cut each in half diagonally once to make 4 triangles (C).
- Cut 4 squares $2\frac{7}{8}''$. Cut each in half diagonally once to make 8 triangles (D).

Dark green

- Cut 4 strips $9'' \times$ a **scant** $2''$.

Dark red

- Cut 4 trapezoids (A).
- Cut 1 square $4\frac{1}{2}''$.

BLOCK ASSEMBLY

1. Sew the 4 golden beige triangles C to the dark red square.

2. Sew 2 of the dark green strips to opposite sides of the central square. Trim the edges even. Sew the remaining dark green strips to the top and bottom of the central unit and trim the edges even.

3. Sew 2 golden beige triangles D to the smallest sides of a dark red A. Sew a golden beige triangle B to the longest side of A to make a corner unit. Make 4 corner units.

4. Sew the 4 corner units to the central unit to complete the block. Press.

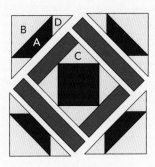

GLAD TIDINGS

CUTTING

Make template A from the pattern on page 47.

Golden beige
- Cut 1 strip 2″ × 14″.
- Cut 8 rectangles 2″ × 3½″.
- Cut 1 square 4¼″. Cut the square in half diagonally twice to make 4 triangles.

Dark green
- Cut 1 strip 2″ × 14″.

Dark red
- Cut 4 parallelograms (A). Flip the template over and cut 4 parallelograms Ar.
- Cut 4 squares 2″.

Gold
- Cut 1 square 3½″.
- Cut 4 squares 2⅜″. Cut each in half diagonally once to make 8 triangles.

BLOCK ASSEMBLY

1. Pair the dark green strip with the golden beige strip, right sides together, and sew along the long sides. Press toward the dark green fabric. Cut 8 segments 2″ wide. Join the segments in pairs to make 4 four-patches.

2. Sew a golden beige rectangle to each four-patch. Sew a dark red square to the end of each remaining rectangle. Sew 1 unit to each four-patch to create a block corner. Make 4 block corners.

Make 4.

3. Sew 1 gold triangle to one end of each red parallelogram A and Ar. Join each A unit with an Ar unit, sewing from point to point only. Using Y-seam construction, set a golden beige triangle F into the angle between the red parallelograms. Make 4.

Make 4.

4. Sew the units into 3 rows. Sew the rows together.

PINE TREE

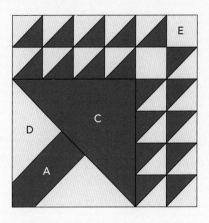

CUTTING

Make template A from the pattern on page 48.

Golden beige
- Cut 1 square 7¾″. Cut the square in half diagonally twice to make 4 triangles (D). Discard 2.
- Cut 2 squares 2½″ (E).
- Cut 9 squares 2⅞″ (B).

Dark green
- Cut 1 trunk (A).
- Cut 9 squares 2⅞″ (B).
- Cut 1 right triangle with 2 sides 8⅞″ (C).

BLOCK ASSEMBLY

1. Referring to Half-Square Triangle Blocks, page 88, make 18 quick-pieced half-square triangle units using the dark green and golden beige squares.

2. Sew the large golden beige triangles D to opposite sides of the trunk A. Sew this unit to the dark green triangle to make the trunk square.

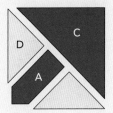

3. Sew each golden beige square to a dark green half-square triangle unit. Sew the 2 units together to make a four-patch.

4. Sew the remaining half-square triangle units into 2 identical rows of 4 and 2 mirror-image rows of 4. Sew the matching rows together along the long sides.

5. Sew 1 of the half-square triangle unit sets to the trunk square. Sew the other half-square triangle unit set to the four-patch.

6. Sew the 2 sections together.

SHEPHERDS' LIGHT

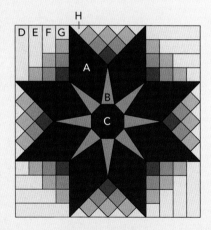

CUTTING

Make templates A, B, and C from the patterns on pages 48–49.

Golden beige
- Cut 4 rectangles $1\frac{3}{8}'' \times 4''$ (D).
- Cut 4 rectangles $1\frac{3}{8}'' \times 3\frac{1}{8}''$ (E).
- Cut 4 rectangles $1\frac{3}{8}'' \times 2\frac{1}{4}''$ (F).
- Cut 4 squares $1\frac{3}{8}''$ (G).
- Cut 4 squares $2\frac{1}{2}''$. Cut each in half diagonally twice to make 16 triangles (H).

Dark green
- Cut 1 strip $1\frac{3}{8}'' \times 14''$.

Medium green
- Cut 4 triangles (B).
- Cut 3 strips $1\frac{3}{8}'' \times 14''$.

Light green
- Cut 2 strips $1\frac{3}{8}'' \times 14''$.
- Cut 4 squares $1\frac{3}{8}''$.

Dark red
- Cut 4 diamonds (A).
- Cut 1 octagon (C) and prepare it according to your favorite appliqué method.

BLOCK ASSEMBLY

1. Sew each dark red diamond A to a medium green triangle B, sewing only to the point at the tip of the star, but through the seam allowance at the base. Sew these units together to make a star-point ring.

2. Appliqué the dark red octagon C to the center of the star-point ring.

3. Sew dark green, medium green, and light green strips together with medium green in the center. From this strip set, cut 8 segments $1\frac{3}{8}''$ wide. Sew a golden beige square to the light green end of 4 segments. Sew a golden beige triangle to the light green end of the remaining 4 segments.

4. Sew a medium green strip and a light green strip together. From this strip set, cut 8 segments $1\frac{3}{8}''$ wide. Sew a $1\frac{3}{8}'' \times 2\frac{1}{4}''$ golden beige rectangle F to the light green end of 4 segments. Sew a golden beige triangle to the light green end of the remaining 4 segments.

5. Sew a golden beige rectangle E to 4 of the light green squares. Sew 2 golden beige triangles to each of the remaining 4 light green squares.

6. Sew together the units with golden beige triangles to make 4 side triangles.

Make 4.

7. Sew together the remaining pieced units to make 4 corner squares.

Make 4.

8. Using Y-seam construction, set the corner square units into the corners of the star-point ring. Set the side triangle units into the remaining angles. Press.

PICTORIAL CENTER

CUTTING

Appliqué template patterns are on pages 49-54.

Dark green
- Cut 2 trees, 4 fleur-de-lis corner pieces, and 16 small leaves.

Medium green
- Cut 2 trees.

Light green
- Cut 1 tree.

Dark red

- Cut 1 cabin, 1 barn, 4 corner branches, and 12 berries and prepare them according to your favorite appliqué method.
- Cut 2 strips 2″ × 24½″.
- Cut 2 strips 2″ × 27½″.

Light blue

- Cut 1 square 26″ for the sky.

White

- Cut 1 ground, 1 background hill, 1 snow for the cabin roof, and 1 snow for the barn roof and prepare them according to your favorite appliqué method.

ASSEMBLY

1. Appliqué the pictorial elements to the 26″ blue sky square, following the quilt assembly diagram on page 44 for placement. After the appliqué is complete, trim the block to 24½″ square (includes seam allowance).

2. Sew the 2 short dark red strips to the sides of the pictorial center. Sew the 2 long dark red strips to the top and bottom of the pictorial center.

DOUBLE SAWTOOTH BORDER

CUTTING

Golden beige

- Cut 90 squares 2⅞″. Set 30 squares aside for making half-square triangle units. Cut the remaining 60 squares in half diagonally once to make 120 small triangles.

Dark green

- Cut 6 squares 4⅞″. Cut each in half diagonally once to make 12 large triangles.
- Cut 6 squares 2⅞″.

Medium green

- Cut 6 squares 4⅞″. Cut each in half diagonally once to make 12 large triangles.
- Cut 6 squares 2⅞″.

Light green

- Cut 6 squares 4⅞″. Cut each in half diagonally once to make 12 large triangles.
- Cut 6 squares 2⅞″.

Dark red

- Cut 6 squares 4⅞″. Cut each in half diagonally once to make 12 large triangles.
- Cut 6 squares 2⅞″.

Gold

- Cut 6 squares 4⅞″. Cut each in half diagonally once to make 12 large triangles.
- Cut 6 squares 2⅞″.

ASSEMBLY

1. Referring to Half-Square Triangle Blocks, page 88, sew the golden beige squares with the squares of other colors to make 12 quick-pieced half-square triangle units in each color: dark red, dark green, medium green, light green, and gold.

2. Sew 2 golden beige triangles to each half-square triangle unit to make a pieced triangle.

3. Varying the colors as desired, sew a large triangle to each pieced triangle set. Make 60 Double Sawtooth squares. Squares should measure 4½″.

Make 60.

4. Sew together 7 Double Sawtooth squares. Make a second, identical row and 2 mirror-image rows. Sew each row of 7 to a mirror-image row so that large triangles touch in the center. Make 2 side borders. Press.

5. Use the same method to make the top and bottom borders, using 8 Double Sawtooth squares in each half row.

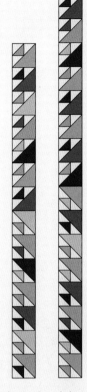

Make 2 of each border.

SASHING, BORDERS, AND QUILT ASSEMBLY

CUTTING

Golden beige

- Cut 6 strips 1½″ for sashing.
- Cut 3 strips 2″ for sashing.
- Cut 6 strips 1″ for inner border.

Dark red

- Cut 16 strips 1″.

ASSEMBLY

1. From the dark red strips, cut 24 strips 12½″ and 24 strips 13½″. Sew a 12½″ strip on 2 opposite sides of each 12″ sampler block. Press. Sew a 13½″ strip on the remaining sides of each block. Press.

2. From the 1½″ sashing strips, cut 8 strips 13½″. Sew the *Christmas Cactus, Star of the Magi, Advent Wreath,* and *Christmas Eve* blocks together, separated by sashing strips, to make the top row. Press.

3. Sew the *Glad Tidings, Manger, Star of Bethlehem,* and *Feathered Star* blocks together, separated by sashing strips, to make the bottom row. Press.

4. Sew the *Shepherds' Light* and *Pine Tree* blocks together vertically, separated by a sashing strip, to make the left side of the middle row. Press. Sew the *Christmas Star* and *Flower of Christmas* blocks together, separated by a sashing strip, to make the right side of the middle row. Press. Sew the left side, pictorial center, and right side together, separated by 27½″ sashing strips, to make the middle row. Press.

5. Sew the 2″ sashing strips together end-to-end and cut 2 strips 55½″. Sew the top, middle, and bottom quilt rows together with a sashing strip between each pair of rows. Press.

6. Sew the 1″ inner border strips together end-to-end and cut 4 strips 56½″. Sew 2 inner borders to the sides of the quilt. Press. Sew the remaining inner borders to the top and bottom of the quilt. Press.

7. Attach the short Double Sawtooth borders to the sides of the quilt. Press.

8. Attach the long Double Sawtooth borders to the top and bottom of the quilt. Press.

9. Referring to Quilting 101, page 88, layer the quilt top, batting, and backing. Baste. Quilt as desired. Attach a hanging sleeve, if desired, and bind with dark red fabric.

Quilt assembly diagram

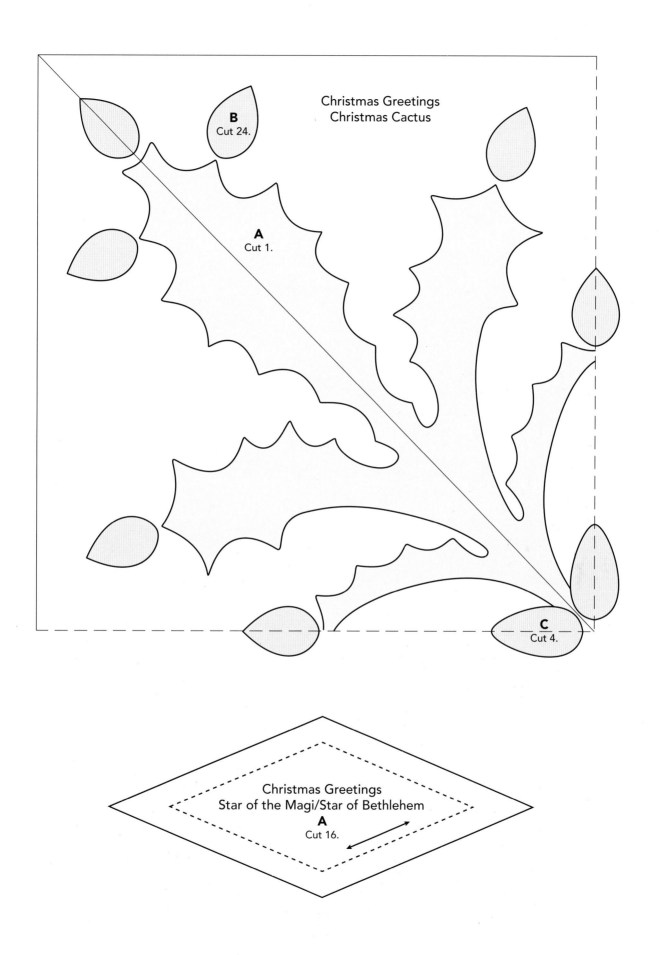

Christmas Greetings
Christmas Cactus

B
Cut 24.

A
Cut 1.

C
Cut 4.

Christmas Greetings
Star of the Magi/Star of Bethlehem

A
Cut 16.

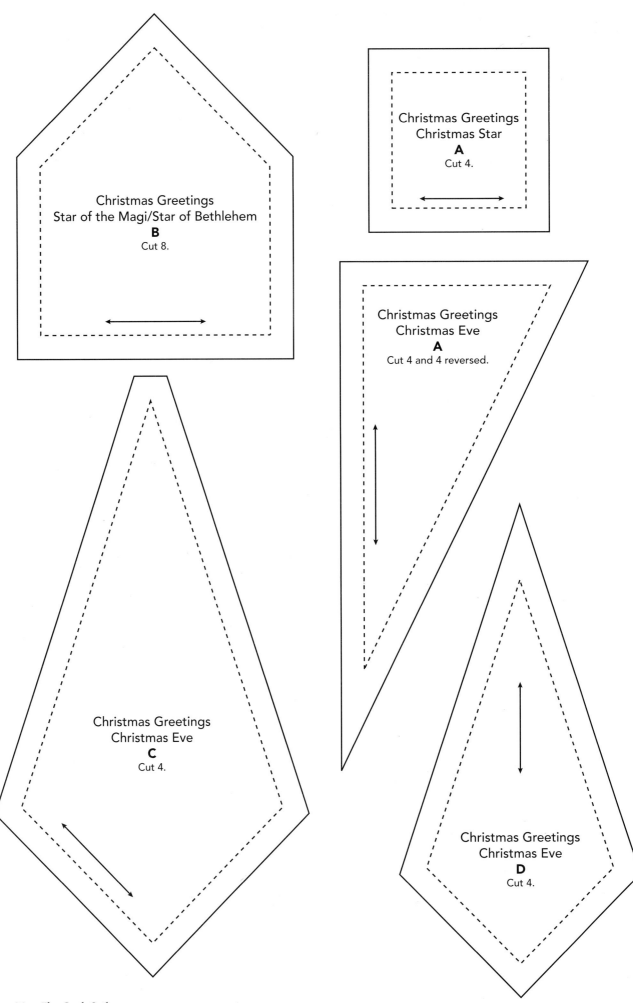

Christmas Greetings
Christmas Star
A
Cut 4.

Christmas Greetings
Star of the Magi/Star of Bethlehem
B
Cut 8.

Christmas Greetings
Christmas Eve
A
Cut 4 and 4 reversed.

Christmas Greetings
Christmas Eve
C
Cut 4.

Christmas Greetings
Christmas Eve
D
Cut 4.

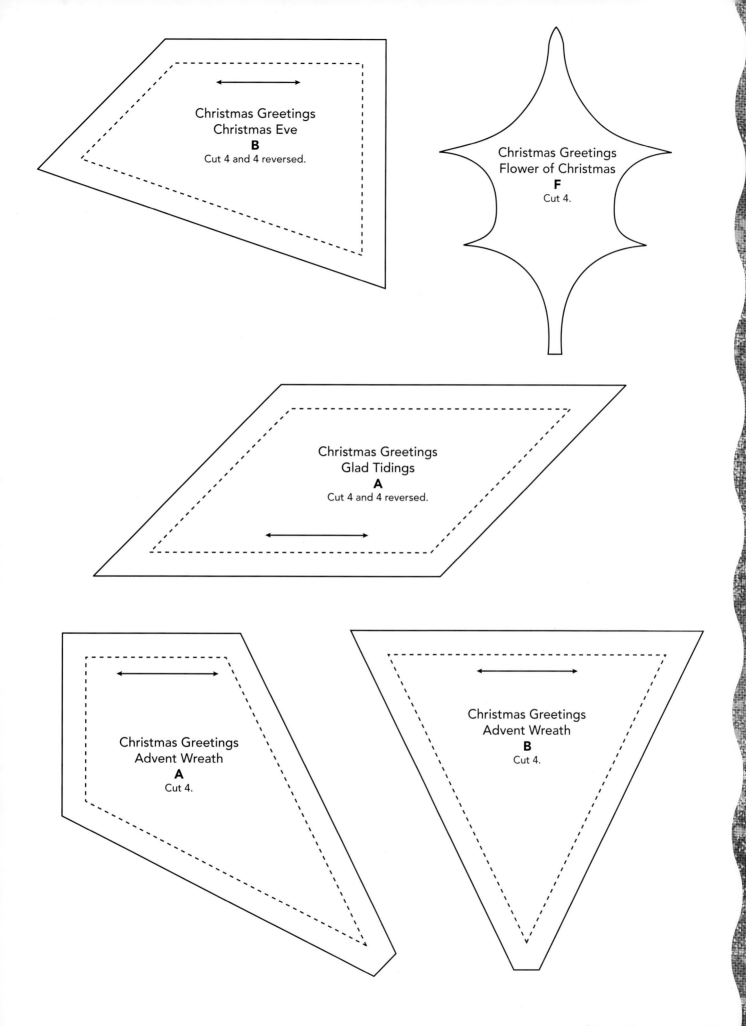

Christmas Greetings
Christmas Eve
B
Cut 4 and 4 reversed.

Christmas Greetings
Flower of Christmas
F
Cut 4.

Christmas Greetings
Glad Tidings
A
Cut 4 and 4 reversed.

Christmas Greetings
Advent Wreath
A
Cut 4.

Christmas Greetings
Advent Wreath
B
Cut 4.

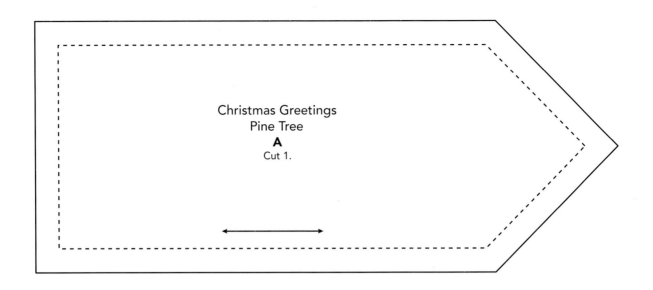

Christmas Greetings
Pine Tree
A
Cut 1.

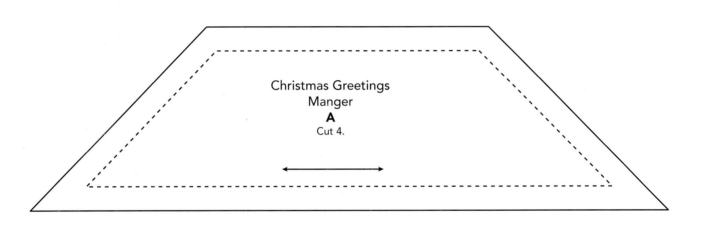

Christmas Greetings
Manger
A
Cut 4.

Christmas Greetings
Shepherds' Light
C
Cut 1.

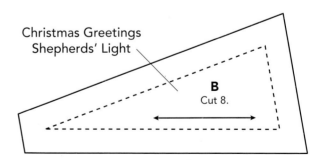

Christmas Greetings
Shepherds' Light
B
Cut 8.

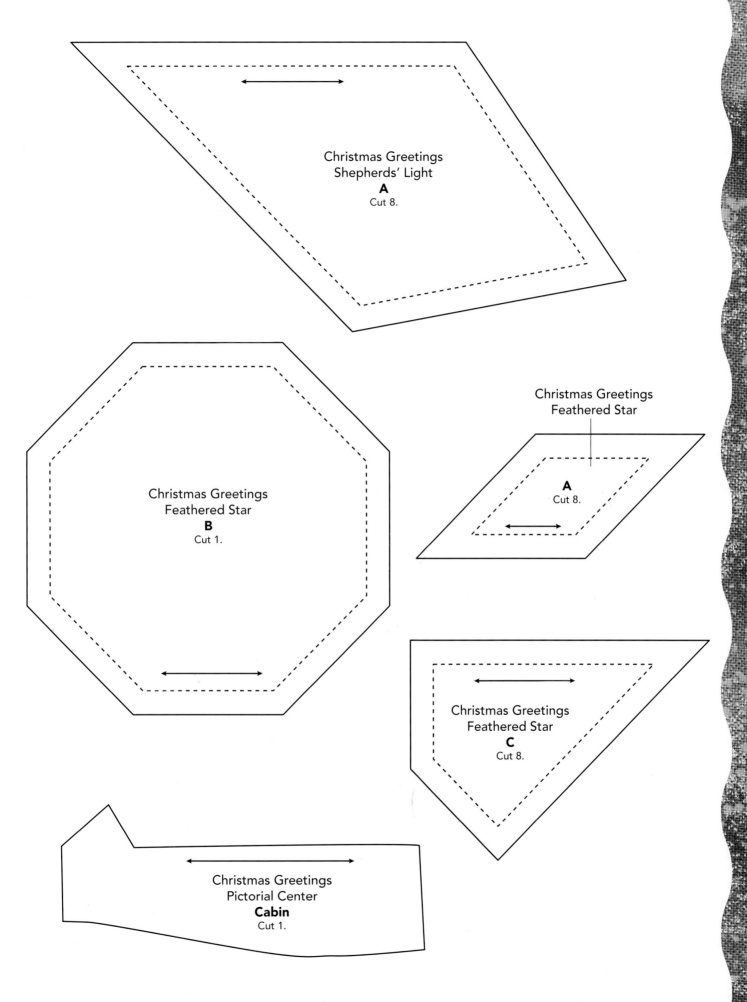

Christmas Greetings
Shepherds' Light
A
Cut 8.

Christmas Greetings
Feathered Star

A
Cut 8.

Christmas Greetings
Feathered Star
B
Cut 1.

Christmas Greetings
Feathered Star
C
Cut 8.

Christmas Greetings
Pictorial Center
Cabin
Cut 1.

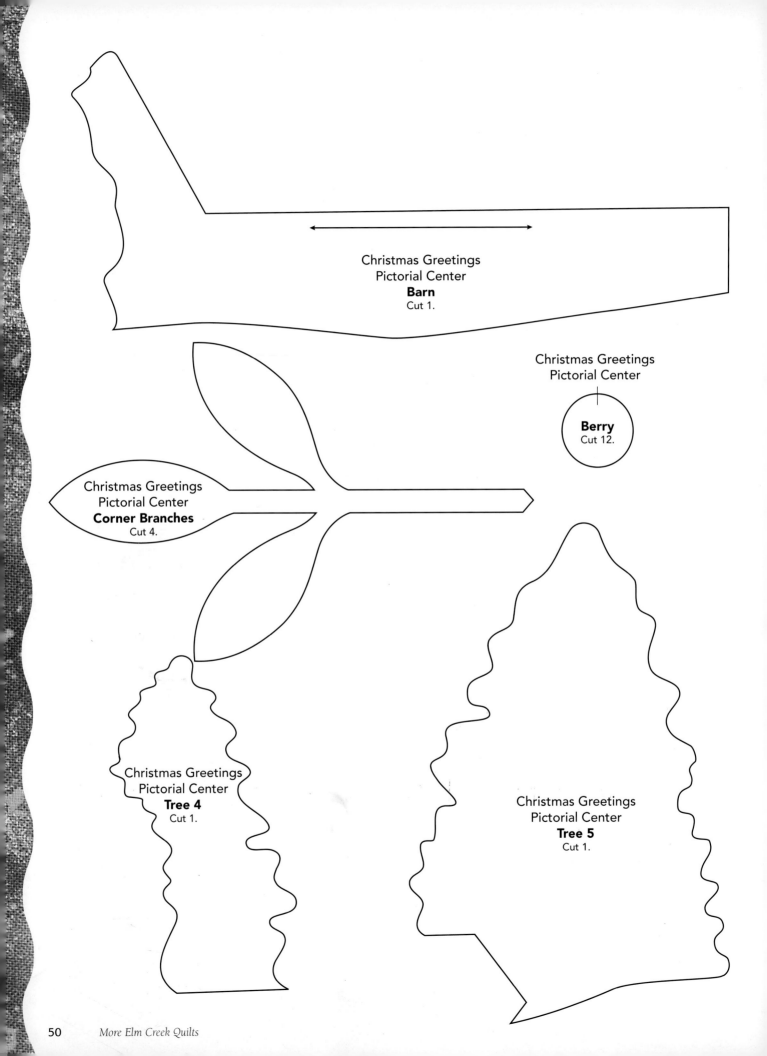

Christmas Greetings
Pictorial Center
Barn
Cut 1.

Christmas Greetings
Pictorial Center

Berry
Cut 12.

Christmas Greetings
Pictorial Center
Corner Branches
Cut 4.

Christmas Greetings
Pictorial Center
Tree 4
Cut 1.

Christmas Greetings
Pictorial Center
Tree 5
Cut 1.

Christmas Greetings
Pictorial Center
Tree 1
Cut 1.

Christmas Greetings
Pictorial Center
Tree 3
Cut 1.

Christmas Greetings
Pictorial Center
Tree 2
Cut 1.

Christmas Greetings
Pictorial Center
Fleur-de-lis
Cut 4.

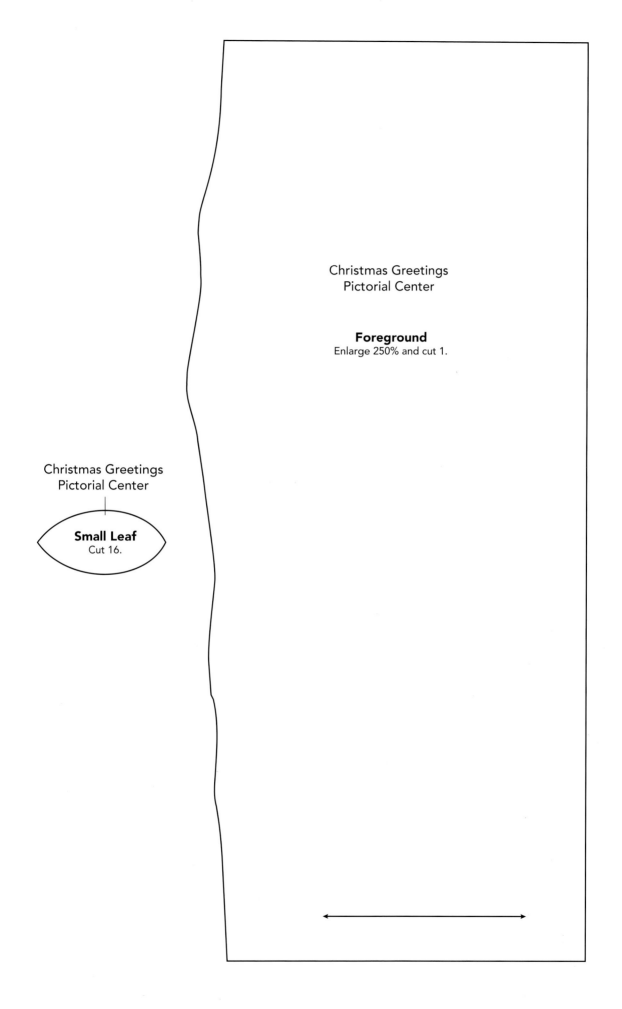

Christmas Greetings
Pictorial Center

Foreground
Enlarge 250% and cut 1.

Christmas Greetings
Pictorial Center

Small Leaf
Cut 16.

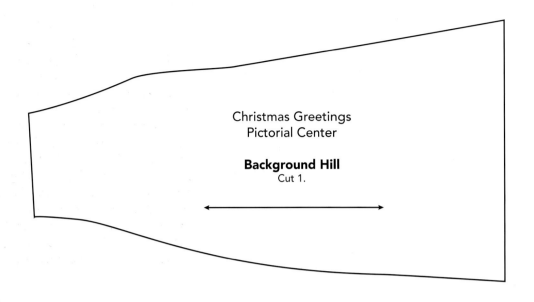

Christmas Greetings
Pictorial Center

Background Hill
Cut 1.

Christmas Greetings
Pictorial Center
Cabin Roof
Cut 1.

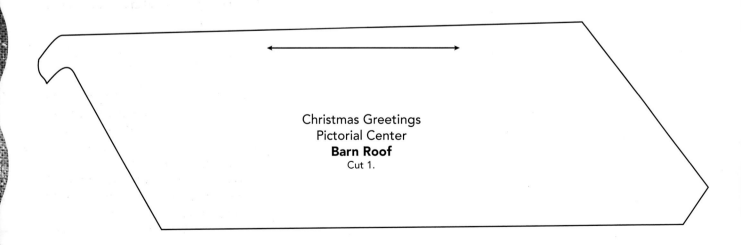

Christmas Greetings
Pictorial Center
Barn Roof
Cut 1.

FROM *Circle of Quilters*

When two of the founding members of Elm Creek Quilt Camp decide to leave the fold, the Elm Creek Quilters face untold changes in their business and tests of the bonds of friendship. Who can possibly fill the empty places within their circle of quilters? An Elm Creek Quilter must possess not only mastery of quilting techniques, but also teaching experience, a sense of humor, and that intangible quality that allows an individual to blend harmoniously into a group. They are seeking not only new teachers to join their staff, but new members of their family.

As quilters everywhere vie to land one of the prestigious posts, Master Quilter Sylvia Compson reminds her friends that they must evaluate all of the applicants' qualities, not only the content of their résumés. Their choice will say as much about them and what they want for the future of Elm Creek Quilts as it says about the qualifications of those they decide to hire.

Circle of Quilters was an especially enjoyable story to tell because it allowed me to explore the lives of five new characters while still portraying the Elm Creek Quilters in important roles. I thrived on delving into these new characters' pasts, discovering their unique quilting interests and the twists and turns in their lives that led them to a love for the art of quilting. The most difficult part of the writing process was deciding who would be offered the jobs, since I had come to know and feel for each character. In fact, I didn't know who would be chosen to join the circle of quilters until I was several paragraphs into the last chapter.

Applicant Maggie Flynn discovers an antique sampler quilt at a garage sale, and not knowing the names of the patterns, she invents her own titles based upon the sparse facts she tracks down about the quilter's past. She takes the Mill Girls name from Harriet Findley Birch's career before her marriage and journey along the Oregon Trail. My mother, Geraldine Neidenbach, sewed this adaptation of Maggie's design using my Elm Creek Quilts: *Dorothea's Collection* fabric line from Red Rooster Fabrics.

Another applicant for the teaching position, Gretchen Hartley, is a staunch traditionalist whose devotion to the tried-and-true often puts her at odds with her quilt shop's senior partner. When she arrives for her interview at Elm Creek Manor, she is astonished to discover a camper working on one of her own original designs, a Dogtooth Violet quilt identical to her own except for the fabric selections. Unraveling the mystery of how her quilt came to be duplicated forces Gretchen to realize that her unscrupulous business partner has been deceiving her.

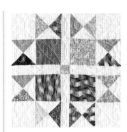

Maggie Flynn

Sacramento resident Maggie Flynn discovers a love for quilting after a bedraggled sampler quilt bought at a garage sale for five dollars turns out to be an antique treasure made by Harriet Findley Birch, a former Lowell mill girl who traveled with her husband along the Oregon Trail in the mid 1800s. As she researches the origins of her find, Maggie becomes a recognized expert on quilt history. The Elm Creek Quilts position opens up just as she faces an impending layoff from her longtime job in geriatric care, prompting her to contemplate a significant life change.

Karen Wise

A loving stay-at-home mom feeling both the joys and the frustrations of her vocation, Karen Wise hopes that her deep understanding of the spirit of Elm Creek Quilts will outweigh her relative inexperience as a quilter. Though she has never taught a quilting class, she is innovative and creative, with a preference for foundation paper-piecing designs and hand-dyed fabrics. Her husband's lack of interest in her dream threatens to sabotage her bid, however, and Karen finds herself torn between the conflicting demands of the interview process and the needs of home.

Anna Del Maso

Quilting is a second love for Anna Del Maso, who sees her position as a Waterford College food services chef as a stepping stone to opening a restaurant of her own one day. She learned to quilt as a teenager working in her aunt's quilt shop, and sees the job at Elm Creek Quilt Camp as a wonderful opportunity to build up her restaurant savings with a second income. Her food-themed quilts are wonderfully innovative, though they fail to impress her snobbish boyfriend.

Russell McIntyre

The only man among the five finalists, Russell McIntyre first took up quilting as a means of mourning his quilter wife who had lost her battle with cancer. Largely self-taught, Russ sidesteps many of the traditions of the craft, but his wholly original, contemporary designs have won him fame. Russ could bring a new perspective to the female-oriented camp, but the gender difference also places him at a disadvantage in the eyes of some key decision-makers at Elm Creek Quilts.

Gretchen Hartley

The oldest of the candidates, Gretchen Hartley sees the job as a means of escape from the thankless circumstances of her position as junior partner at a Sewickley quilt shop. As one of Sylvia's first quilting pupils, Gretchen helped keep quilting traditions alive in the decades before the "quilting renaissance" of the late 1970s. After her husband suffers a serious injury at work in a Pittsburgh steel mill, Gretchen supports the family on her salary as a substitute teacher. A place among the circle of quilters at Elm Creek Manor would be the fulfillment of a dream and a well-deserved reward for a lifetime of hard work.

A month after Maggie submitted her portfolio, Sarah McClure from Elm Creek Quilt Camp called with an invitation to come to Pennsylvania for an interview. As a test of her skills and creativity, Maggie was also instructed to design an original quilt block that could be used as a logo for Elm Creek Quilts. She was so thrilled to have an interview that she would have agreed to anything. She adapted two of Harriet Findley Birch's patterns, a leaf design and a star, and overlaid them to create a new block. Imitating Harriet's flowing script, in one corner of the block she embroidered "Elm Creek Quilts" and in another, "Waterford, Penn."

Throughout the years, Harriett had often felt like a guardian spirit to Maggie, lingering just beyond her vision, offering wisdom, encouragement, sympathy, understanding. Maggie wondered what Harriet would make of her pinning all her hopes on a job on the other side of the country. Perhaps more than anyone else, she would have understood.

—Excerpted from *Circle of Quilters* by Jennifer Chiaverini

When it was [Gretchen's] turn to leaf through the pages [of the first quilting magazine], she felt a stirring of excitement and belonging that she had not felt since that long ago home economics education course in college, with the admired instructor who was as passionate about precise piecing as she was about the storied heritage of American quilting. For so many years she had felt that her love for quilting isolated her until at last she discovered a small group of likeminded friends. Now she realized that they were not alone, that they were part of a larger community, a circle of quilters that had kept quilting alive and were passing along their skill and wisdom as generations of women had before them.

—Excerpted from *Circle of Quilters* by Jennifer Chiaverini

VIOLETS FOR GRETCHEN

From *Circle of Quilters* by Jennifer Chiaverini

FINISHED SIZE: 74″ × 74″
FINISHED BLOCK SIZE: 11⅝″ × 11⅝″
NUMBER OF BLOCKS: 24
Machine pieced by Rita DeMarco, machine quilted by Anne Smith, 2007.

FABRIC REQUIREMENTS

- **Purple:** 4½ yards (includes border and binding)
- **Dark gold:** 1½ yards
- **Green:** ¾ yard
- **Red:** ⅜ yard
- **Light gold:** 4¼ yards
- **Batting:** 78″ × 78″
- **Backing:** 4⅝ yards

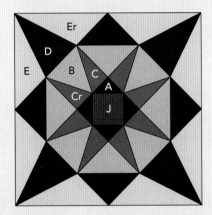

CUTTING

Make templates B, D, E, F, G, H, and J from the patterns on pages 60–61.

Purple
- Cut 48 squares 2¼″. Cut each in half diagonally once to make 96 triangles (A).
- Cut 48 squares 3⅝″.
- Cut 96 triangles (D).
- Cut 16 triangles (F). Flip the template over and cut 16 Fr.
- Cut 9 strips 4½″ by the width of the fabric for the border.

Dark gold
- Cut 48 squares 3⅝″.
- Cut 96 triangles (B).

Green
- Cut 96 rectangles 2″ × 4″. Cut 48 rectangles in half diagonally once from lower left to upper right to make 96 triangles (C). Cut the remaining 48 rectangles in half diagonally once from lower right to upper left to make 96 triangles (Cr).

Red
- Cut 24 squares (J).

Light gold
- Cut 96 triangles (E). Flip the template over and cut 96 triangles Er.
- Cut 16 triangles (G).
- Cut 16 triangles (H). Flip the template over and cut 16 Hr.
- Cut 4 squares 12¼″. Cut each in half diagonally twice to make 16 triangles (I).

BLOCK ASSEMBLY

1. Referring to Half-Square Triangle Blocks, page 88, make 96 quick-pieced half-square triangle units using the dark gold and purple 3⅝″ squares.
2. Sew 4 purple triangles A to each red square to make a square-in-a-square unit. Press. Make 24.

Make 24.

3. Sew 1 green C and 1 green Cr to each dark gold B. Press. Make 96.

Make 96.

4. Sew 2 half-square triangle units and a C/B/Cr unit into a row. Make 48 rows.

Make 48.

5. Sew 2 C/B/Cr units and 1 square-in-a-square unit into a row. Make 24 rows.

Make 24.

6. Sew 2 of the rows created in Step 4 to opposite sides of 1 of the rows created in Step 5. Make 24 block centers.

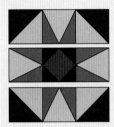

Make 24.

7. Sew light gold triangles E and Er to a purple triangle D to make a block corner. Make 96.

Make 96.

8. Sew 2 block corners to opposite sides of 1 block center. Press. Sew 2 more block corners to the remaining sides. Press. Make 24 Dogtooth Violet blocks.

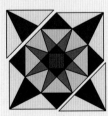

Make 24.

QUILT ASSEMBLY

1. Sew 1 light gold H to 1 purple F.
Sew 1 light gold Hr to 1 purple Fr.
Sew both units to 1 light gold G.
Attach 1 light gold I. Make 16
pieced border triangles.

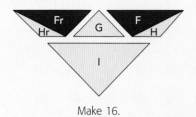

Make 16.

2. Sew the Dogtooth Violet blocks and
pieced border triangles into diagonal rows. Press.

3. Sew the rows together, pressing
after each addition.

4. Sew the purple border strips
together end-to-end and cut 4 strips
4½″ × 80″. (**Note:** *Always measure
your quilt top and adjust the lengths of
your borders if necessary.*) Referring
to Mitered Borders, page 90, sew
the purple border strips to the quilt.

5. Referring to Quilting 101, page 88,
layer the quilt top, batting, and
backing. Baste. Quilt as desired.
Attach a hanging sleeve, if desired,
and bind with purple fabric.

Quilt assembly diagram

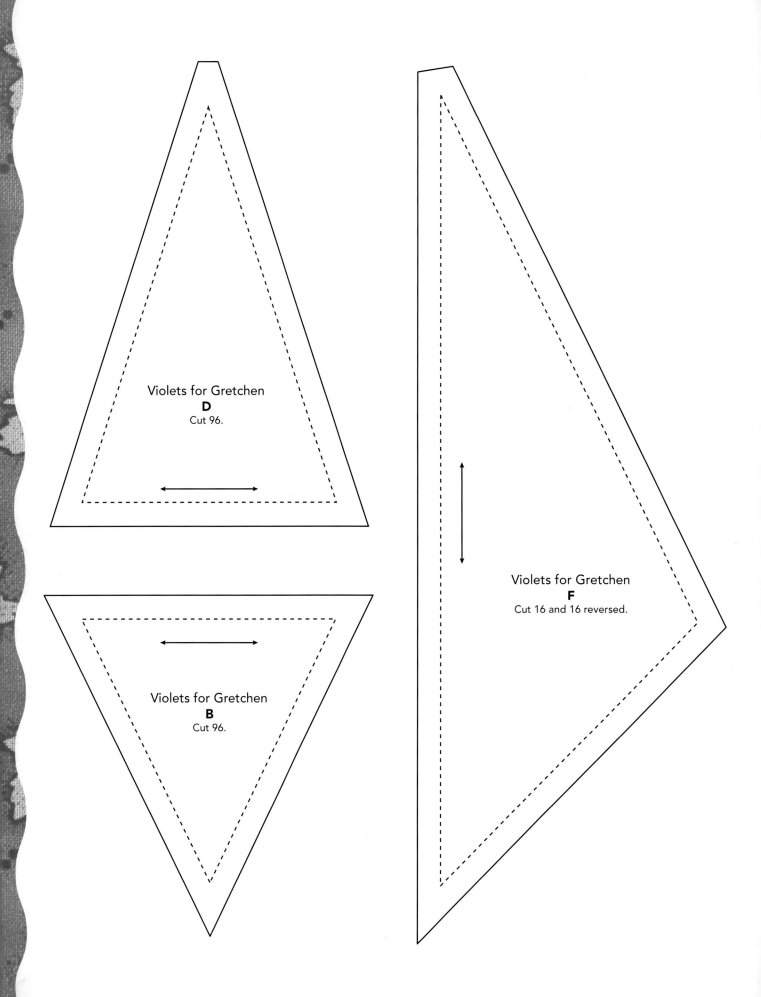

Violets for Gretchen
D
Cut 96.

Violets for Gretchen
B
Cut 96.

Violets for Gretchen
F
Cut 16 and 16 reversed.

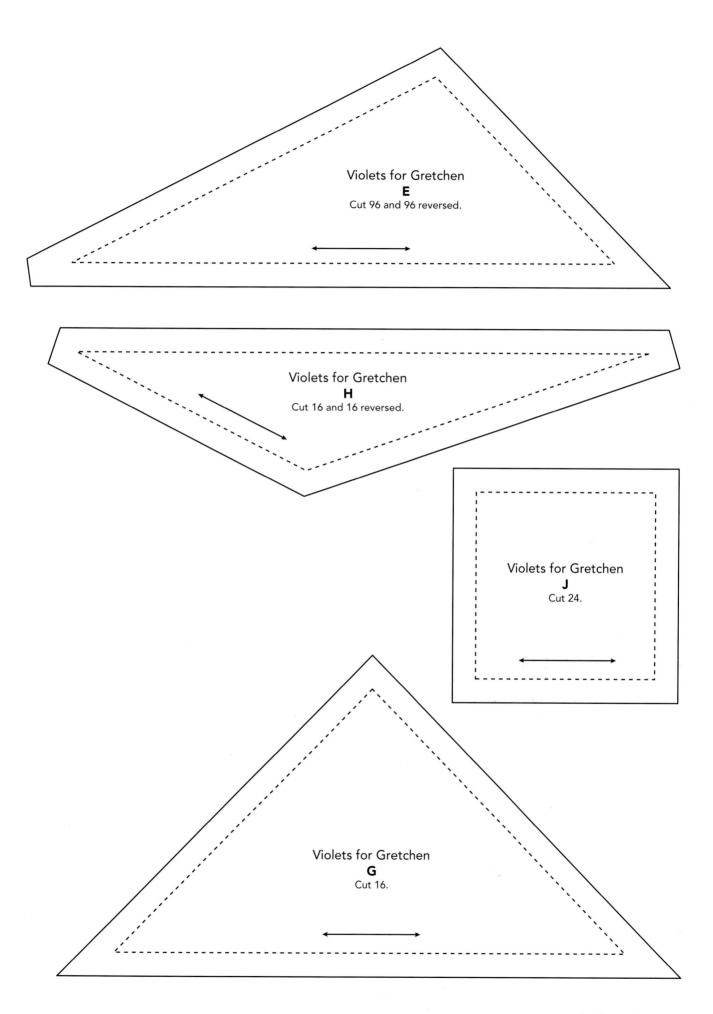

Violets for Gretchen
E
Cut 96 and 96 reversed.

Violets for Gretchen
H
Cut 16 and 16 reversed.

Violets for Gretchen
J
Cut 24.

Violets for Gretchen
G
Cut 16.

MILL GIRLS

From *Circle of Quilters* by Jennifer Chiaverini

FINISHED SIZE: 64″ × 80″
FINISHED BLOCK SIZE: 12″ × 12″
NUMBER OF BLOCKS: 20
Machine pieced by Geraldine Neidenbach, machine quilted by Sue Vollbrecht, 2006.

FABRIC REQUIREMENTS

- **Assorted green prints:** 1 yard total
- **Assorted blue prints:** 1 yard total
- **Assorted yellow prints:** 1 yard total
- **Assorted purple prints:** 1 yard total
- **Assorted pink prints:** 1 yard total
- **Light beige tone-on-tone:** $4\frac{1}{2}$ yards (includes sashing and border)
- **Dark blue:** $\frac{3}{4}$ yard for binding
- **Batting:** $68'' \times 84''$
- **Backing:** $4\frac{3}{4}$ yards

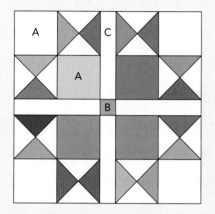

CUTTING

Assorted green, blue, yellow, purple, and pink prints:

Cut the following from **each** color family:

- 16 squares 4" (80 squares total)
- 16 squares $3\frac{1}{4}$" (A; 80 squares total)
- 4 squares $1\frac{1}{2}$" (B; 20 squares total)
- 7 squares $5\frac{1}{4}$" for the pieced border (35 squares total)

Light beige tone-on-tone

- Cut 80 squares 4".
- Cut 80 squares $3\frac{1}{4}$" (A).
- Cut 80 rectangles $1\frac{1}{2}$" × 6" (C).
- Cut 15 block sashing strips $2\frac{1}{2}$" × $12\frac{1}{2}$".
- Cut 9 strips $2\frac{1}{2}$" for the row sashing.
- Cut 4 strips $1\frac{1}{2}$" for the inner border.
- Cut 35 squares $5\frac{1}{4}$" for the pieced border.

BLOCK ASSEMBLY

1. Referring to Half-Square Triangle Blocks, page 88, make 160 quick-pieced quarter-square triangle units using the 4" print squares, paired with the 4" light beige squares.
2. Sew 80 quarter-square triangle units to light beige squares A and 80 to print squares A. Sew each beige square unit to a print square unit to make a block quarter. Make 80.

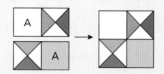

Make 80.

3. Sew 2 block quarters to opposite sides of a light beige rectangle C. Make 40 block halves.
4. Sew the remaining light beige rectangles C to opposite sides of the $1\frac{1}{2}$" print squares B.
5. Sew a block half to each side of a sashing unit created in Step 4. Make 20 blocks.

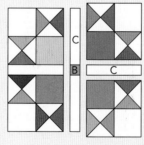

Make 20.

QUILT ASSEMBLY

1. Sew the blocks into 5 rows of 4 blocks, separating each pair of blocks with light beige sashing strips. Press the seams toward the sashing strips.

2. Sew the row sashing strips together end-to-end and cut 6 strips $2\frac{1}{2}$" × $54\frac{1}{2}$". Sew the rows of blocks together, separating each pair of rows with sashing strips. Add row sashing strips to the top and bottom of the quilt. Press the seams toward the sashing strips.
3. Sew the inner-border strips together end-to-end and cut 2 strips $1\frac{1}{2}$" × $72\frac{1}{2}$". Sew the inner borders to the sides of the quilt. Press. (**Note:** Always measure your quilt top and adjust the lengths of your borders if necessary.)
4. Use the $5\frac{1}{4}$" squares to make 70 quick-pieced quarter-square triangle units. Make 2 borders of 18 triangle units each and sew the borders to the sides of the quilt, referring to the assembly diagram on page 64 for position. Make 2 borders of 16 quarter-square triangle units each and sew the borders to the top and bottom of the quilt. (You will have 2 quarter-square triangle units left over.) Press the seams away from the pieced borders.
5. Referring to Quilting 101, page 88, layer the quilt top, batting, and backing. Baste. Quilt as desired. Attach a hanging sleeve, if desired, and bind with dark blue fabric.

Quilt assembly diagram

FROM *The Quilter's Homecoming*

In 1925, Elizabeth Bergstrom Nelson leaves Elm Creek Manor with her new husband, Henry, for the adventure of a lifetime. They hold the deed to Triumph Ranch, one hundred twenty acres of prime California soil located in the Arboles Valley north of Los Angeles. In a cruel reversal of fortune, the Nelsons arrive to the news that they've been swindled, and they are left suddenly, irrevocably penniless. Hiring on as hands at the farm they thought they owned, Henry struggles with his pride, but clever, feisty Elizabeth draws on her share of the Bergstrom women's inherent economy and resilience and vows to defy fate.

The Chimneys and Cornerstones quilt that Elizabeth receives as a wedding gift from her Great-Aunt Lucinda made its first appearance in *The Quilter's Apprentice*. The members of my online community, the Elm Creek Readers, generously contributed all of the beautiful blocks using two variations of the traditional pattern.

Antique quilts I discovered at the Stagecoach Inn Museum in Newbury Park, California, while researching *The Quilter's Homecoming* inspired the two other quilts featured in the novel. My sister, Heather Neidenbach, pieced the octagonal *Road to Triumph Ranch* quilt, which Elizabeth discovers in the ramshackle cabin that becomes the Nelsons' home. Pat Morris pieced and quilted *Arboles Valley Star*, which Elizabeth names in honor of her new home. I thoroughly enjoyed writing *The Quilter's Homecoming*, not only because my research led me to such lovely antiques, but also because the Arboles Valley is loosely based upon the Conjeo Valley, where I once lived.

Elizabeth Bergstrom Nelson

Though she was raised in Harrisburg, Pennsylvania, rather than Elm Creek Manor, Elizabeth considers the Bergstrom family estate the true home of her heart and visits as often as she can. Beautiful, spirited, and clever, Elizabeth often acts without thinking but can usually charm her way out of trouble. She is Sylvia's favorite cousin, and the younger girl is heartbroken when Elizabeth and Henry announce their plans to marry and move to California, where Elizabeth faces the first real test of her resourcefulness and moral courage.

Henry Nelson

The grandson of Dorothea and Thomas Nelson, Henry's roots in the Elm Creek Valley run even deeper than the Bergstroms', which makes his decision to leave the Nelson family farm for a California ranch all the more surprising. Hardworking and steadfast, Henry secretly wonders whether Elizabeth married him out of love or because his family's farm lies adjacent to Elm Creek Manor, which she longs for but cannot have.

Isabel Rodriguez Diaz

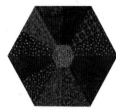

Born in 1870 on El Rancho Triunfo in southern California, Isabel learns heartbreak at an early age when her family is forced to sell their once-prosperous lands after suffering through a lengthy drought. She is fifteen when her mother's death forces her to leave school to care for her younger brother and sister. Despite the blessings of a loving marriage and two beloved children, throughout her life Isabel mourns the loss of the ranch—and she cannot forgive those who she believes stole it from the Rodriguez family.

Rosa Diaz Barclay

Isabel is determined to give her eldest child and only daughter every opportunity she herself was denied, but headstrong, passionate Rosa heeds her own heart rather than her mother's prudent counsel. As a young woman she is torn between two rivals for her affection: a hardworking if temperamental local farmer who offers her security, and a man who truly loves her but is drawn to drink—and belongs to the family who now owns the Rodriguez land, the family her mother despises.

Elizabeth unfolded the wedding quilt and spread it upon her lap, pride a warm glow in her chest as Mrs. Diegel exclaimed in awe and delight over the Bergstrom women's handiwork… Elizabeth was pleased and comforted by Mrs. Diegel's declaration that they were the two most beautiful and well-made quilts she had ever seen.

"Your family clearly takes pride in their work," she said. As Elizabeth thanked her and folded the quilts, Mrs. Diegel added, "What will you take for them?"

Elizabeth let out a small laugh of surprise. "Sorry, nothing. I couldn't part with them."

"Surely there's something else you need."

"Not more than I need these quilts."

"I have a copper bathtub left over from before we had indoor plumbing. It's been in storage in the carriage house for years. Polish it up a bit and it will be as good as new."

Elizabeth hesitated, but shook her head. "I'm sorry, but no."

"Oh, come now," said Mrs. Diegel. "A young girl like yourself, a new bride no less, and you're willing to go without a good soak in the tub at the end of a long day?"

Elizabeth closed her eyes, the quilts a soft, comforting weight in her arms. She could almost feel the steam rise from the hot bath, feel the water enveloping her, bubbles tickling her toes. Then she opened her eyes. "I'm sorry. It's not enough."

—Excerpted from *The Quilter's Homecoming* by Jennifer Chiaverini

Elizabeth's gaze fell upon the worn scrap quilt she had found in the cabin. It had held up well to washing, but she had paid little attention to it since then except to feel grateful each night for the warmth it provided. It was wrinkled and faded, especially compared to the quilts she had given up, but now that she studied it more carefully, she could not help admiring the ingenious design. She had never seen a star pattern quite like it before, despite the hundreds of quilts she had witnessed the Bergstrom women make through the years…

Elizabeth wondered who had made it. Mrs. Jorgensen's grandmother, perhaps, or could the quilt be even older than that? It seemed to be pieced of scraps of clothing, which always made it more difficult to date. Had the fading and wear to the fabric occurred before or after the pieces were sewn into a quilt? Perhaps the quilt had been made far away and brought to the Arboles Valley by a young bride trusting in her husband's decision to bring her out West far from home and family, trusting that he would always cherish her and never give her reason to regret her decision.

—Excerpted from *The Quilter's Homecoming* by Jennifer Chiaverini

LUCINDA'S GIFT

From *The Quilter's Homecoming* by Jennifer Chiaverini

FINISHED SIZE: 56″ × 70″
FINISHED BLOCK SIZE: 7″ × 7″
NUMBER OF BLOCKS: 48 Variation 1, 32 Variation 2
Machine pieced by Jennifer Chiaverini and the Elm Creek Readers, machine quilted by Sue Vollbrecht, 2006.

FABRIC REQUIREMENTS

- **Assorted reds:** 1½ yards total
- **Assorted blues and greens (darks):** 2½ yards total
- **Assorted creams and light beiges (lights):** 2½ yards total
- **Dark blue:** ⅝ yard for binding
- **Batting:** 60″ × 74″
- **Backing:** 3½ yards

VARIATION 1

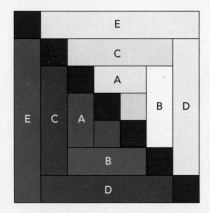

CUTTING

Reds
- Cut 336 squares 1½″.

Blues and greens (darks)
- Cut 48 squares 1½″.
- Cut 48 rectangles 1½″ × 2½″ (A).
- Cut 48 rectangles 1½″ × 3½″ (B).
- Cut 48 rectangles 1½″ × 4½″ (C).
- Cut 48 rectangles 1½″ × 5½″ (D).
- Cut 48 rectangles 1½″ × 6½″ (E).

Creams and light beiges (lights)
- Follow the cutting directions for the dark fabrics.

BLOCK ASSEMBLY

1. Pair 1 red square with a light square and sew them together. Pair 1 red square with a dark square and sew them together. Sew the square pairs together to make a four-patch.

2. Sew 1 red square to the end of each light rectangle A, B, C, D, and E.
3. Following the block diagram for color placement, sew a dark A rectangle to the center four-patch created in Step 1.
4. Sew dark B, C, D, and E rectangles and light/red pieced units to opposite sides of the center unit in order of increasing size. Make 48 Variation 1 blocks.

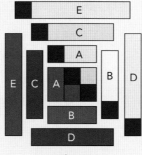

Make 48.

VARIATION 2

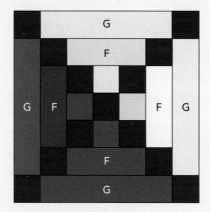

CUTTING

Reds
- Cut 416 squares 1½″.

Blues and greens (darks)
- Cut 64 squares 1½″.
- Cut 64 rectangles 1½″ × 3½″ (F).
- Cut 64 rectangles 1½″ × 5½″ (G).

Creams and light beiges (lights)
- Follow the cutting directions for the dark fabrics.

BLOCK ASSEMBLY

1. Sew 5 red squares, 2 light squares, and 2 dark squares into a Nine-Patch by sewing the squares into 3 rows and then sewing the rows together. Follow the diagram below for color placement.

2. Sew 2 red squares to opposite ends of 1 light rectangle F and 1 light rectangle G to make 1 short light strip and 1 long light strip. Repeat with a dark rectangle F and a dark rectangle G to make 1 short dark strip and 1 long dark strip.

3. Following the block diagram for color placement, sew a light F rectangle and a dark F rectangle to opposite sides of the Nine-Patch created in Step 1.
4. Sew light and dark F and G rectangles and the short and long F and G rectangle strips to opposite sides of the Nine-Patch. Make 32 Variation 2 blocks.

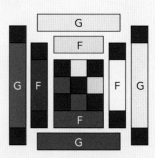

Make 32.

QUILT ASSEMBLY

1. Sew 8 Variation 2 blocks together to make the top row. Press. Repeat to make the bottom row.

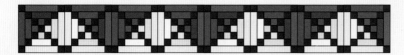

2. Sew 6 Variation 1 blocks together. Sew a Variation 2 block to each end to complete the row. Press. Make 8 rows.

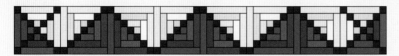

3. Arrange the rows as shown in the quilt assembly diagram below. Sew the 10 rows together, pressing after each addition.

4. Referring to Quilting 101, page 88, layer the quilt top, batting, and backing. Baste. Quilt as desired. Attach a hanging sleeve, if desired, and bind with dark blue fabric.

Quilt assembly diagram

CONTRIBUTING QUILTERS

Valerie Almas
Tanya Anderson
Yvonne Bagnell
Colleen Bartell
Rose M. Bezuk
Karen Brasher
Pamela Bruner
Kathy Cather
Trisha Chubbs
Sue Chura
Kathleen Clary-Cooke
Dot Colna
Angie Copija-Crosson
Annice Peckham Crandall
Dottie Creeron
Judy Cuthbertson
Simone de Haan
Marilyn Dickson
Nancy Erwin
Katherine Fenn
Sandy Findlay
Shirley Flowers
Joanne Flynn-Watson

Debbie K. Frey
Jan Gobeille
Ruth Green
Karen Hallman
Sandi Harrah
Patricia J. Harrell
Sue Harris
Barb Hartwig
Pam Henrys
Hester Huiskamp
Tina Jacobson
Barbara Jennekens
Katrina Kahn
Francine C. Kennedy
Sandie Larsen
Pam Leach
Therese Lecluyse
Karen Katsumi Mantione
Sandra McLay
Sheri L. Meerscheidt
Trish Miller
Fannie C. Narte
Mary Nice

Becca Olson
Sharon R. Pasma
Patricia Rahrig
Francisca L. Reit
Michele Ringenberg
Lynette Root
Cheryl Samp
Judy Scollay
Shannon Shaw
Louise Smith
Toni A. Spear
Mary Joy Speicher
Julie Gilman Spokane
Shelley Stevens
Barbara Sundloff-Wilson
Ginny Svatek
Fran Threewit
Jeane Stewart Tucker
Annelies van den Bergh
Anita van der Spek
Jaine Pancoast Vaughn
Diane Wilshere

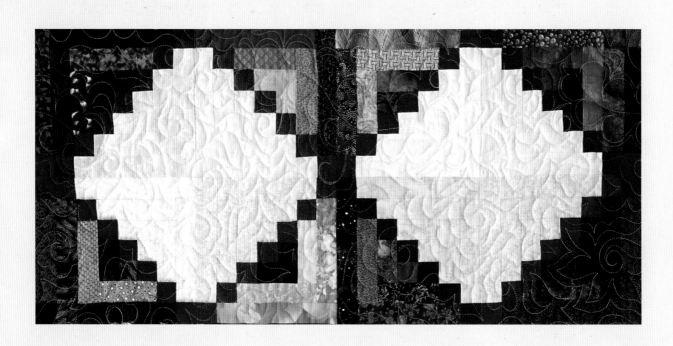

ROAD TO TRIUMPH RANCH

From *The Quilter's Homecoming* **by Jennifer Chiaverini**

FINISHED SIZE: 65½″ × 92″
FINISHED BLOCK SIZE: Hexagons with 10″ sides
NUMBER OF BLOCKS: 14 hexagons, 10 half-hexagons, 4 quarter-hexagons
Machine pieced by Heather Neidenbach, machine quilted by Sue Vollbrecht, 2006.

FABRIC REQUIREMENTS

- **Greens:** 3¾ yards (includes outer border and binding)
- **Purples:** assorted fat quarters, 2 yards total
- **Wines:** assorted fat quarters, 2 yards total
- **Blues:** assorted fat quarters, 2 yards total
- **Rusts:** assorted fat quarters 2 yards total
- **Gold:** ¾ yard
- **Batting:** 70″ × 96″
- **Backing:** 5½ yards

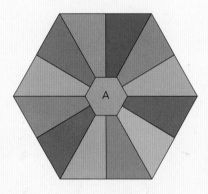

CUTTING

Make template A from the pattern on page 73.

Wines, purples, greens, blues, and rusts

- Cut 24 rectangles 5¾″ × 9⅞″ from each color family for a total of 120 rectangles.

Gold

- Cut 28 hexagons (A) and prepare them according to your favorite appliqué method.

Green

- Cut 8 strips 3″ for the border.

BLOCK ASSEMBLY

1. Cut 12 rectangles of each color in half diagonally from the lower left corner to the upper right corner to make 24 triangles of each color. Cut the remaining 12 rectangles of each color in half diagonally from the lower right corner to the upper left corner to make mirror-image triangles. You will have a total of 120 triangles and 120 mirror-image triangles.

2. Sew the triangles together in groups of 3 to make 40 hexagon-quarters and 40 mirror-image hexagon-quarters. Arrange the colors so that 2 hexagon-quarters and 2 mirror-image hexagon-quarters are composed of only green triangles. Repeat to make 2 blue hexagon-quarters and 2 blue mirror-image hexagon-quarters and 2 purple hexagon-quarters and 2 purple mirror-image hexagon-quarters. The remaining units should be made from a random arrangement of colors.

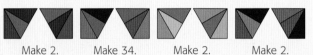

Make 2. Make 34. Make 2. Make 2.

3. Sew each green hexagon-quarter to a mirror-image green hexagon-quarter. Sew the 2 halves together to make 1 hexagon. Repeat with the blue and purple hexagon-quarters and mirror-image hexagon-quarters.

4. Set 2 multicolored hexagon-quarters and 2 mirror-image multicolored hexagon-quarters aside. Sew each remaining multicolored hexagon-quarter to a mirror-image multicolored hexagon-quarter to make 32 halves.

5. Set 10 of the multicolored hexagon-halves aside. Join the remaining halves to make 11 multicolored hexagon blocks.

6. Appliqué a gold hexagon A to the center of each pieced hexagon block.

QUILT ASSEMBLY

1. Join the pieced hexagon blocks, half-hexagons, and quarter-hexagons into 5 vertical rows, as shown in the quilt assembly diagram. (**Note:** *Sew from point to point only, not into the seam allowances.*)

2. Using Y-seam construction, sew the 5 rows together.

3. Sew the green border strips together end-to-end and cut 2 strips 3″ × 87″ and 2 strips 3″ × 65½″. (**Note:** *Always measure your quilt top and adjust the lengths of your borders if necessary.*)

4. Attach the long borders to the sides of the quilt. Press. Attach the short borders to the top and bottom of the quilt. Press.

5. Appliqué the remaining gold hexagons A to the centers of the half-hexagons and the quarter-hexagons. The appliqués should overlap the quilt borders.

6. Referring to Quilting 101, page 88, layer the quilt top, batting, and backing. Baste. Quilt as desired. Attach a hanging sleeve, if desired, and bind with green fabric.

Quilt assembly diagram

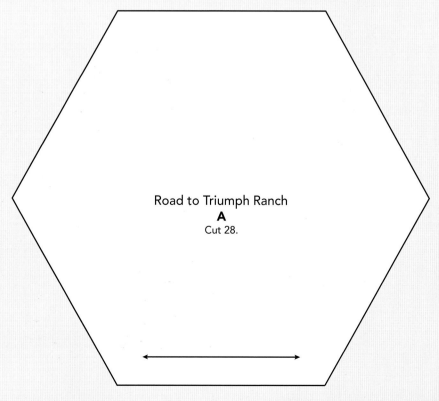

Road to Triumph Ranch
A
Cut 28.

ARBOLES VALLEY STAR

From *The Quilter's Homecoming* **by Jennifer Chiaverini**

FINISHED SIZE: 68″ × 92″
FINISHED BLOCK SIZE: 12″ × 12″
NUMBER OF BLOCKS: 35
Machine pieced and quilted by Pat Morris, 2007.

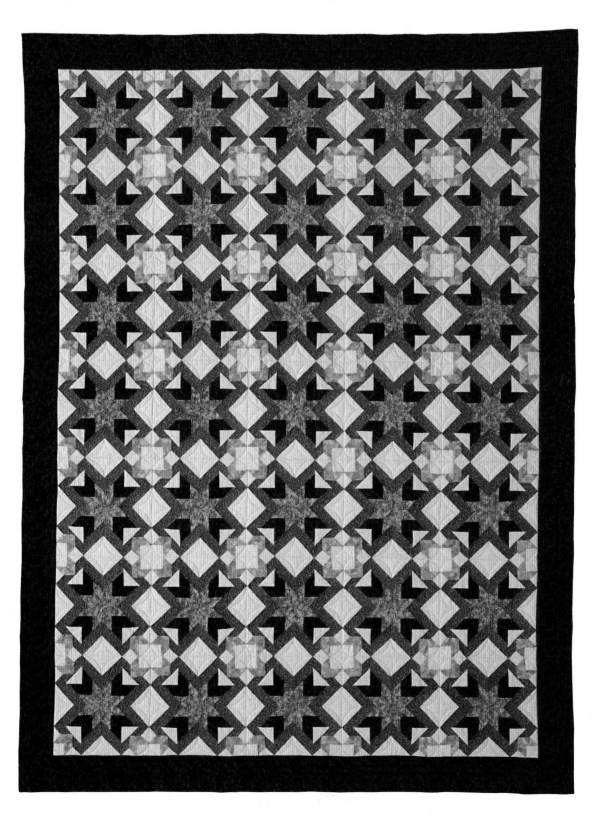

FABRIC REQUIREMENTS

- **Red:** 2¾ yards (includes border and binding)
- **Green:** 3 yards
- **Pink:** 1¼ yards
- **Gold:** 1 yard
- **Cream:** 4¾ yards
- **Batting:** 72″ × 96″
- **Backing:** 5½ yards

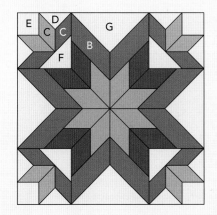

CUTTING

Make templates B, C, D, E, F, and G from the patterns on page 77.

Red
- Cut 19 strips 1¾″ by the width of fabric.
- Cut 8 strips 4½″ by the width of fabric for the border.

Green
- Cut 140 parallelograms (B). Flip the template over and cut 140 parallelograms Br.
- Cut 280 diamonds (C).

Pink
- Cut 19 strips 1¾″.

Gold
- Cut 280 diamonds (C).

Cream
- Cut 280 triangles (D).
- Cut 140 squares (E).
- Cut 140 triangles (F).
- Cut 140 triangles (G).

BLOCK ASSEMBLY

1. Pair each red strip with a pink strip and sew the strips together along their long edges. With a rotary cutter, trim off one end of the strip pair at a 45° angle. Cut 140 segments 1¾″ wide and 140 mirror-image segments 1¾″ wide to make diamond pairs A and Ar.

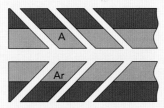

Make 140 of each.

2. Sew 1 green parallelogram B to each diamond pair A to make 140 star points. Repeat with each diamond pair Ar to make 140 mirror-image star points.

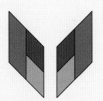

Make 140.

3. Stitching from point to point only, sew each star point to a mirror-image star point. Make 140 star-point pairs.

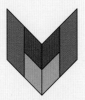

Make 140.

4. Stitching from point to point only, sew each green diamond C to a gold diamond C to make 140 diamond pairs and 140 mirror-image diamond pairs.

Make 140 of each.

5. Referring to Y-Seam Construction, page 88, set a cream triangle D into each green/gold diamond pair.

Make 140 of each.

6. Sewing from point to point only, attach 1 cream square E to the gold diamond of each green/gold diamond pair. Using Y-seam construction, sew each of these units to a mirror-image green/gold diamond pair.

Make 140.

7. Sew 1 cream triangle F to each of the units created in Step 6 to make 140 block corners.

Make 140.

8. Using Y-seam construction, set a block corner into each of the star-point pairs created in Step 3. Make 140.

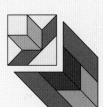

Make 140.

9. Sewing from point to point only, sew 1 cream triangle G to each unit created in Step 8. Using Y-seam construction, join the units into pairs to make 70 block halves.

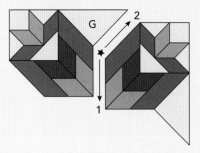

Make 70.

10. Using Y-seam construction, sew together 2 block halves to complete 1 Arboles Valley Star block. Make 35.

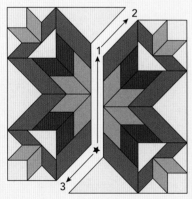

Make 35.

QUILT ASSEMBLY

1. Sew the blocks into 7 rows of 5 blocks each. Press.

2. Sew the 7 rows together. Press.

3. Sew the red border strips together end-to-end and cut 2 strips $4\frac{1}{2}'' \times 84\frac{1}{2}''$ and 2 strips $4\frac{1}{2}'' \times 68\frac{1}{2}''$. (***Note:*** *Always measure your quilt top and adjust the lengths of your borders if necessary.*) Sew the long borders to the sides of the quilt. Sew the short borders to the top and bottom of the quilt.

4. Referring to Quilting 101, page 88, layer the quilt top, batting, and backing. Baste. Quilt as desired. Attach a hanging sleeve, if desired, and bind with red fabric.

Quilt assembly diagram

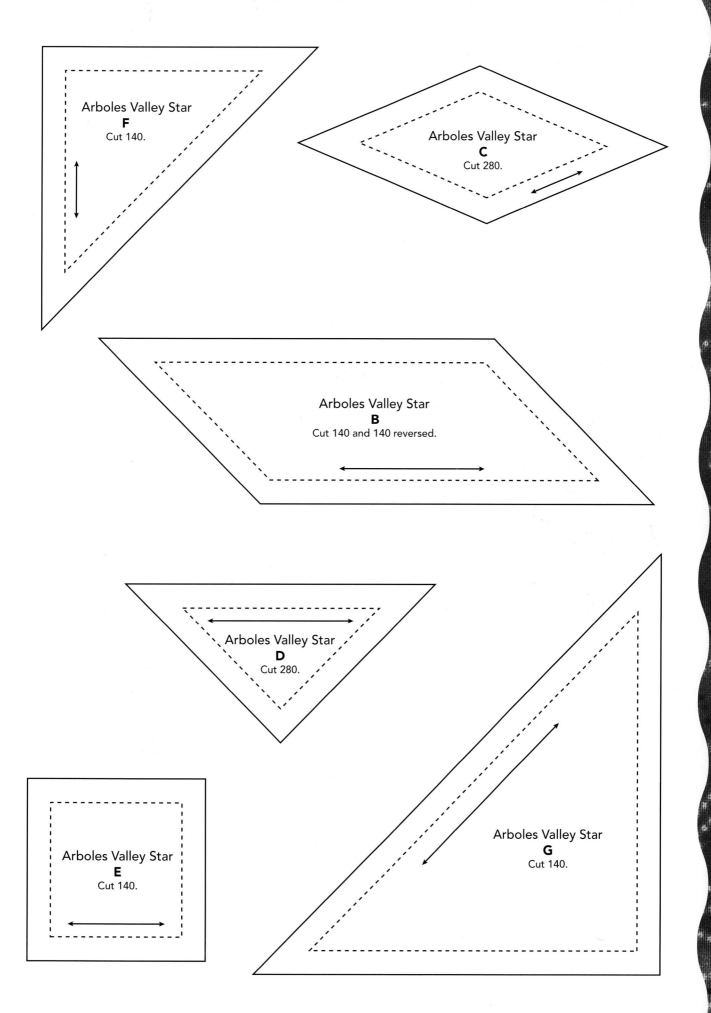

Arboles Valley Star
F
Cut 140.

Arboles Valley Star
C
Cut 280.

Arboles Valley Star
B
Cut 140 and 140 reversed.

Arboles Valley Star
D
Cut 280.

Arboles Valley Star
E
Cut 140.

Arboles Valley Star
G
Cut 140.

FROM *The New Year's Quilt*

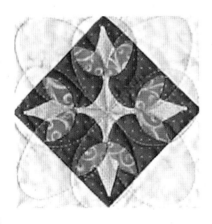

At the close of *The Quilter's Legacy*, my fifth novel, the Elm Creek Quilters gathered with their families to celebrate Christmas Eve at Elm Creek Manor, where they were surprised yet overjoyed to witness the wedding of Sylvia and her beloved Andrew.

The New Year's Quilt tells the story of how the newlyweds celebrate their first holiday season as husband and wife. Not content to rest at home by the fire, they set out on a journey across the snow-covered fields of Pennsylvania. They first enjoy a honeymoon stay at a Manhattan bed-and-breakfast inn owned by Adele Crosier, an Elm Creek Quilts camper, but their ultimate destination is Connecticut, and the home of Andrew's daughter, Amy. Unlike the Elm Creek Quilters, Amy has not offered her blessing to the union. Though her father has reminded her that marriage endures in sickness and in health, Amy fears that Andrew and Sylvia have passed the age where marriage remains a prudent choice.

Sylvia hopes to win over her new daughter-in-law through the lessons that quilting reveals about the bonds of love and family. As a gift for Amy, she undertakes a quilt titled *New Year's Reflections*, whose blocks represent the holiday traditions of Elm Creek Manor. As she stitches the blocks, memories of a lifetime come flooding back, along with words of wisdom meant to celebrate the achievements of generations past and create hope for the future.

Although readers might have expected *The New Year's Quilt* to immediately follow *The Christmas Quilt*, I decided to set it later in the chronology of Elm Creek Manor because Sylvia and Andrew's Christmas Eve wedding seemed the perfect occasion to launch a new story. Also, ever since *The Quilter's Legacy* was published, readers have asked me whether the couple's plans to reconcile with Amy over the holiday week came to fruition. *The New Year's Quilt* offered me the perfect opportunity to answer readers' lingering questions while also celebrating the New Year's traditions of the Bergstrom family in a new holiday tale.

Andrew Cooper

Andrew Cooper has admired Sylvia from the time he was her younger brother's boyhood friend. When Andrew and Sylvia reunite after a long separation, their friendship soon grows into mutual affection, and then blossoms into love. He asks Sylvia several times to marry him before she finally agrees, moved by revelations from the journal of her great-grandfather's sister, Gerda Bergstrom, not to let love pass her by. Andrew enjoys the outdoors and travel, and his favorite pastime is fishing. A true gentleman, he is astonished and troubled when his grown children do not welcome the news of his engagement to Sylvia.

Amy Cooper Lonsdale

Andrew's eldest daughter resides with her husband and two children in a historic Queen Anne home in Hartford, Connecticut. A beginning quilter, she takes to Sylvia's lessons eagerly—until Sylvia becomes engaged to her father. Although her father and younger brother might describe her as headstrong and perhaps even bossy, she prefers to consider herself well-organized and born to lead. Amy is devoted to her family, but she resists change and cherishes mementos of days gone by. Her favorite holiday is Christmas—but her least favorite is New Year's Eve.

Adele Crosier

A former Wall Street trader, Adele is prompted by crisis to leave her high-powered, high-stress career for a new life as the owner of a bed-and-breakfast on Manhattan's Upper East Side. Adele enjoys exploring her artistic talents, and dabbles in quilting, composing poetry, and writing the history of the original owners of her historic brownstone home. She and her husband, a history professor at Hunter College, take pride in making their guests feel like true New Yorkers no matter how brief their stay in the city.

Josephine Compson

Sylvia's mother in-law is a wise and loving woman who, like her husband, celebrates her son James's happiness when he marries Sylvia and welcomes her into the family with great joy. Upon James's death in World War II, Josephine offers Sylvia comfort and sanctuary at the Compson farm on the Chesapeake Bay in Maryland, and gently encourages her to build a new life for herself. She longs for Sylvia to reconcile with her estranged sister, Claudia, and believes Sylvia's rightful place is home at Elm Creek Manor.

Sylvia methodically sewed down the binding, each stitch bringing her closer to the completion of the quilt she had titled "New Year's Reflections." Out of the corner of one eye, she observed Andrew frowning slightly as he pondered the mystery of her quilt's presence on their honeymoon. "Did you bring the quilt because last year you resolved to finish it before midnight on New Year's Eve, and you're running out of time?"

"No," said Sylvia, with a little laugh. "I brought it along because it's a gift for Amy."

"But we sent the kids their Christmas presents weeks ago."

"It's not a Christmas gift. It's a New Year's gift." Sylvia hesitated before deciding to tell him the whole truth. He was, after all, her husband now. "It's a gift to thank her for accepting my marriage to her father."

Andrew shot her a look of utter bewilderment. "But she didn't," he said, quickly returning his gaze to the road ahead. "She doesn't. She made that perfectly clear when I told her I was going to marry you whether she liked it or not. Sylvia, I think you should prepare yourself. This peace offering of yours—it's a pretty quilt and a nice gesture, but it might not be enough. This whole trip might be a waste of time."

"I refuse to believe that," said Sylvia. Their attempt to reconcile with Amy was for them as much as it was for her. It would do them some small good to know they had tried, even if Amy rebuffed them.

And while it was true that Amy had not accepted her father's engagement and almost certainly would not welcome news of his marriage, perhaps by the time the New Year dawned, she would have a change of heart. Sylvia would put her trust in the power of the season to inspire new beginnings, even if Andrew did not.

—Excerpted from *The New Year's Quilt* by Jennifer Chiaverini

NEW YEAR'S REFLECTIONS

From *The New Year's Quilt* by Jennifer Chiaverini

FINISHED SIZE: 60″ × 60″
FINISHED BLOCK SIZE: 12″ × 12″
NUMBER OF BLOCKS: 12 (Each Mother's Favorite block has a different 4″ block center.)
Machine pieced by Christie Batterman, machine quilted by Elaine Beattie, 2007.

FABRIC REQUIREMENTS

- **Dark blue:** 1½ yards (includes binding)
- **Light blue:** 1¼ yards
- **Dark gold:** ½ yard
- **Light gold:** ¼ yard
- **Ivory:** 4½ yards
- **Batting:** 68″ × 68″
- **Backing:** 4 yards

PINWHEEL

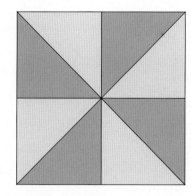

CUTTING

Light blue
- Cut 2 squares 2⅞″.

Light gold
- Cut 2 squares 2⅞″.

BLOCK ASSEMBLY

1. Referring to Half-Square Triangle Blocks, page 88, make 4 quick-pieced half-square triangle units using the light blue and light gold squares.
2. Sew gold/blue half-square triangle units together as shown.

GOOD FORTUNE

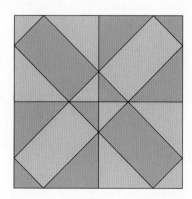

CUTTING

Light blue
- Cut 2 rectangles 1¾″ × 2½″.
- Cut 2 squares 2½″. Cut each in half diagonally once to make 4 large triangles.
- Cut 2 squares 1¾″. Cut each in half diagonally once to make 4 small triangles.

Dark gold
- Follow the cutting directions for the light blue fabric.

BLOCK ASSEMBLY

1. Piece 2 of foundation paper-piecing pattern A, page 87, following the block assembly diagram for color placement. Make 2 more with the color placement reversed.
2. Sew 1 A to a reverse A. Repeat to make 2 block halves.
3. Sew the 2 halves together. Press.

BRIGHT HOPES

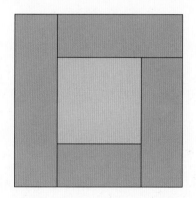

CUTTING

Light blue
- Cut 1 rectangle 1½″ × 2½″.
- Cut 2 rectangles 1½″ × 3½″.
- Cut 1 rectangle 1½″ × 4½″.

Dark gold
- Cut 1 square 2½″.

BLOCK ASSEMBLY

Working from the shortest rectangle to the longest, sew the light blue rectangles to the dark gold square, Log Cabin fashion. Press.

PEACE AND PLENTY

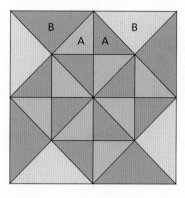

CUTTING

Light blue
- Cut 2 squares 2⅝″. Cut each in half diagonally twice to make 8 small triangles (A).
- Cut 1 square 3¼″. Cut the square in half diagonally twice to make 4 large triangles (B).

Dark gold
- Cut 2 squares 2⅝″. Cut each in half diagonally twice to make 8 small triangles (A).

Light gold
- Cut 1 square 3¼″. Cut the square in half diagonally twice to make 4 large triangles (B).

BLOCK ASSEMBLY

1. Sew each light blue triangle A to a dark gold triangle A. Join these units into pairs to make 4 quarter-square triangle units.
2. Following the block assembly diagram for color placement, join the quarter-square triangle units together in pairs. Press. Sew the pairs together to make the central unit. Press.
3. Sew each light blue triangle B to a light gold triangle B to make 4 corner triangles.

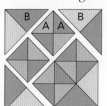

4. Sew the corner triangles to the central unit. Press.

WANDERING FOOT

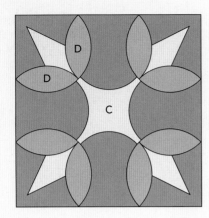

CUTTING

Appliqué template patterns are on page 86.

Light blue

- Cut 1 square 4½″. (**Note:** *You may wish to cut your square larger and trim it to 4½″ square after completing the appliqué.*)

Dark gold

- Cut 8 ovals (D) and prepare them according to your favorite appliqué method.

Light gold

- Cut 1 (C) and prepare it according to your favorite appliqué method.

BLOCK ASSEMBLY

1. Fold the light blue square in half horizontally, vertically, and twice diagonally, pressing after each fold to mark the square's center and to create placement lines.
2. Following the block diagram for correct placement, appliqué C to the background square.
3. Appliqué the D pieces in place.

MEMORY CHAIN

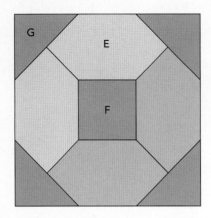

CUTTING

Make template E from the pattern on page 86.

Light blue

- Cut 1 square 1¾″ (F).
- Cut 2 squares 2¼″. Cut each in half diagonally once to make 4 light blue triangles (G).

Dark gold

- Cut 2 hexagons (E).

Light gold

- Cut 2 hexagons (E).

BLOCK ASSEMBLY

1. Referring to Y-Seam Construction, page 88, sew from point to point only to add 1 dark gold E and 1 light gold E to opposite sides of the light blue square F. Press.
2. Sew the remaining E pieces to opposite sides of F and then to the adjacent E pieces. Press.
3. Sew the light blue corner triangles G to the central unit. Press.

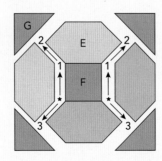

TRUE LOVER'S KNOT

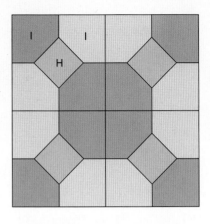

CUTTING

Make templates H and I from the patterns on page 86.

Light blue

- Cut 8 (I).

Dark gold

- Cut 4 squares (H).

Light gold

- Cut 8 (I).

BLOCK ASSEMBLY

1. Referring to Y-Seam Construction, page 88, sew from point to point only to add 2 light gold I pieces to opposite sides of each dark gold square H. Press.
2. Sew the light blue I pieces to opposite sides of the dark gold square H and then to the adjacent light gold I pieces. Press.
3. Following the block assembly diagram, join the units in pairs. Press.
4. Sew the pairs together. Press.

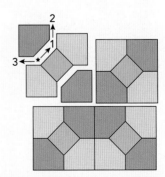

YEAR'S FAVORITE

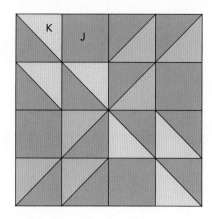

CUTTING

Light blue

- Cut 4 squares $1\frac{1}{2}''$ (J).
- Cut 6 squares $1\frac{7}{8}''$ (K).

Dark gold

- Cut 3 squares $1\frac{7}{8}''$ (K).

Light gold

- Cut 3 squares $1\frac{7}{8}''$ (K).

BLOCK ASSEMBLY

1. Referring to Half-Square Triangle Blocks, page 88, make 6 light gold/light blue half-square triangle units and 6 dark gold/light blue half-square triangle units.
2. Sew the half-square triangle units and light blue squares J into 4 rows, as shown in the block assembly diagram below. Press.
3. Sew the 4 rows together. Press.

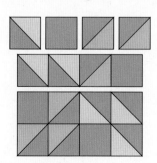

ORANGE PEEL

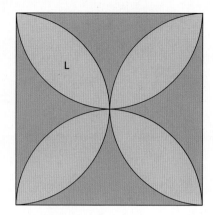

CUTTING

Appliqué template pattern is on page 87.

Light blue

- Cut 1 square $4\frac{1}{2}''$. (**Note:** *You may wish to cut your square larger and trim it to $4\frac{1}{2}''$ square after completing the appliqué.*)

Dark gold

- Cut 4 ovals (L) and prepare them according to your favorite appliqué method.

BLOCK ASSEMBLY

1. Fold the light blue square in half horizontally, vertically, and twice diagonally, pressing after each fold to mark the square's center and to create placement lines.
2. Following the block diagram, appliqué the L pieces to the background square.

FOUR-PATCH

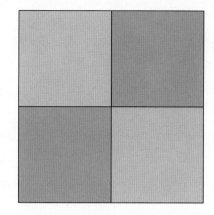

CUTTING

Light blue

- Cut 3 squares $2\frac{1}{2}''$.

Dark gold

- Cut 2 squares $2\frac{1}{2}''$.

BLOCK ASSEMBLY

1. Sew a dark gold square to a light gold square. Repeat.
2. Sew the pairs together with opposite colors facing each other. Press.

HATCHET

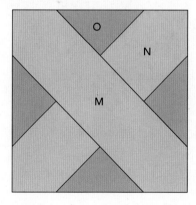

CUTTING

Make templates M and N from the patterns on page 87.

Light blue

- Cut 1 square $3\frac{1}{4}''$. Cut the square in half diagonally twice to make 4 light blue triangles (O).

Dark gold

- Cut 1 hexagon (M).
- Cut 2 pentagons (N).

BLOCK ASSEMBLY

1. Sew 2 light blue triangles to opposite sides of an N piece. Press. Repeat.
2. Sew the pieced corner triangles to opposite sides of the M piece. Press.

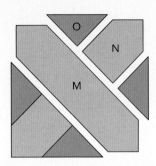

RESOLUTION SQUARE

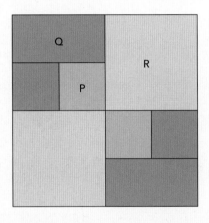

CUTTING

Light blue
- Cut 2 squares 1½″ (P).
- Cut 2 rectangles 1½″ × 2½″ (Q).

Dark gold
- Cut 2 squares 1½″ (P).

Light gold
- Cut 2 squares 2½″ (R).

BLOCK ASSEMBLY

1. Sew each light gold square P to a light blue square P. Press.
2. Sew each P/P pair to a light blue rectangle Q. Press.
3. Sew a P/P/Q unit to a light gold square R to make 1 row. Press. Repeat.

4. Sew the 2 rows together.

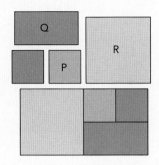

MOTHER'S FAVORITE

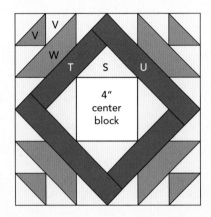

CUTTING

Make templates T and U from the patterns on page 87.

Light blue
- Cut 24 squares 3¼″. Cut each in half diagonally once to make 48 triangles (V).
- Cut 48 rectangles 2½″ × 6½″ (W).

Dark blue
- Cut 24 rectangles (T).
- Cut 24 rectangles (U).

Ivory
- Cut 12 squares 5¼″. Cut each in half diagonally twice to make 48 large triangles (S).
- Cut 120 squares 3¼″. Cut each in half diagonally once to make 240 small triangles (V).

BLOCK ASSEMBLY

1. Sew 2 large ivory triangles S to opposite sides of one of the pieced 4″ center blocks. Press. Sew 2 more large ivory triangles S to the remaining sides. Press.

2. Sew 2 short light blue rectangles T to opposite sides of the unit from Step 1. Press. Sew 2 long light blue rectangles U to the top and bottom of each unit. Press.
3. Use 4 light blue and 20 ivory triangles V and 4 rectangles W to piece 4 foundation paper-piecing pattern X corner units.
4. Sew 2 corner units to opposite sides of the unit from Step 2. Press. Sew 2 more corner units to the remaining sides. Press.
5. Repeat Steps 1–4 to make a total of 12 Mother's Favorite blocks, each with a different 4″ center block.

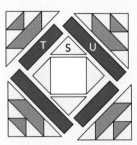

PIECED BORDERS

CUTTING

Light blue
- Cut 24 rectangles 2½″ × 6½″ (W).

Dark gold
- Cut 12 squares 3¼″. Cut each in half diagonally once to make 24 triangles (V).

Ivory
- Cut 60 squares 3¼″. Cut each in half diagonally once to make 120 small triangles (V).
- Cut 5 squares 9¾″. Cut each in half diagonally once to make 20 triangles (Y).

ASSEMBLY

1. Use the light blue, dark gold, and ivory triangles V and W to make 24 triangle units of foundation paper-piecing pattern X, page 86.

2. Sew together 6 paper-pieced triangle units and 5 ivory triangles Y to make 1 border. Press. Make 4 borders.

QUILT ASSEMBLY

CUTTING

Ivory

- Cut 1 square $18\frac{1}{4}$". Cut in half diagonally twice to make 4 triangles (Z).
- Cut 2 squares $17\frac{7}{8}$". Cut each in half diagonally once to make 4 triangles (AA).

- Cut 2 squares $9\frac{3}{8}$". Cut each in half diagonally once to make 4 corner triangles (BB). (**Note:** *Handle all the triangles carefully to avoid distorting the bias edges.*)

ASSEMBLY

1. Sew the Mother's Favorite blocks, Z triangles, and AA triangles into 3 diagonal rows, as shown in the quilt assembly diagram. Press. Sew the rows together. Press.

2. Sew 2 of the pieced borders to the sides of the quilt. Press. Sew the remaining borders to the top and bottom of the quilt. Press.

3. Sew the ivory triangles BB to the corners of the quilt. Press.

4. Referring to Quilting 101, page 88, layer the quilt top, batting, and backing. Baste. Quilt as desired. Attach a hanging sleeve, if desired, and bind with dark blue fabric.

Quilt assembly diagram

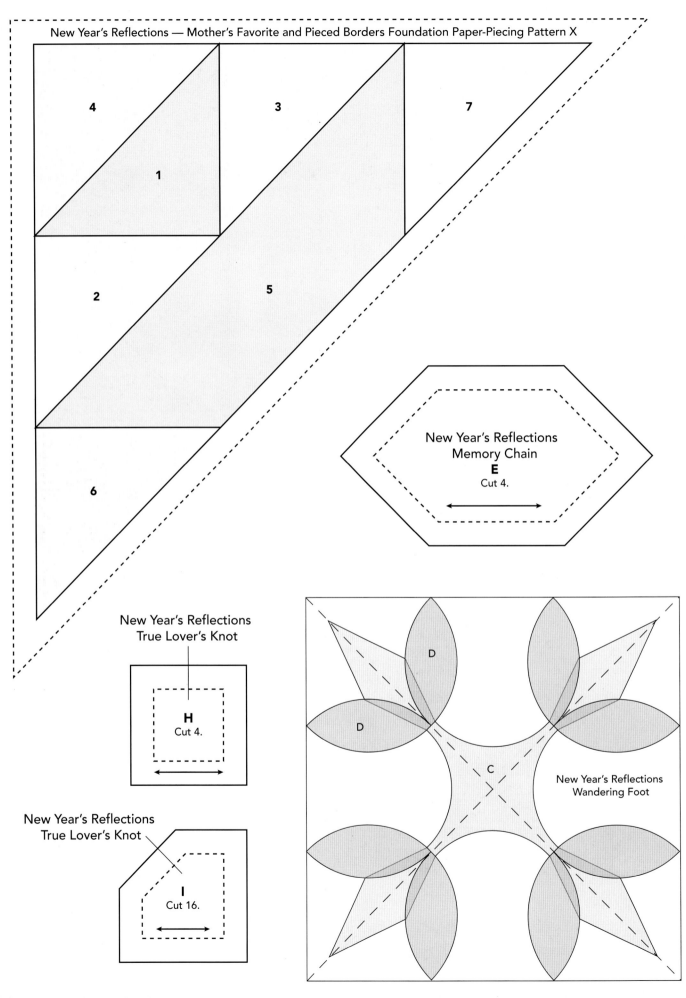

New Year's Reflections — Mother's Favorite and Pieced Borders Foundation Paper-Piecing Pattern X

4

1

3

7

2

5

6

New Year's Reflections
Memory Chain
E
Cut 4.

New Year's Reflections
True Lover's Knot

H
Cut 4.

New Year's Reflections
True Lover's Knot

I
Cut 16.

D

D

C

New Year's Reflections
Wandering Foot

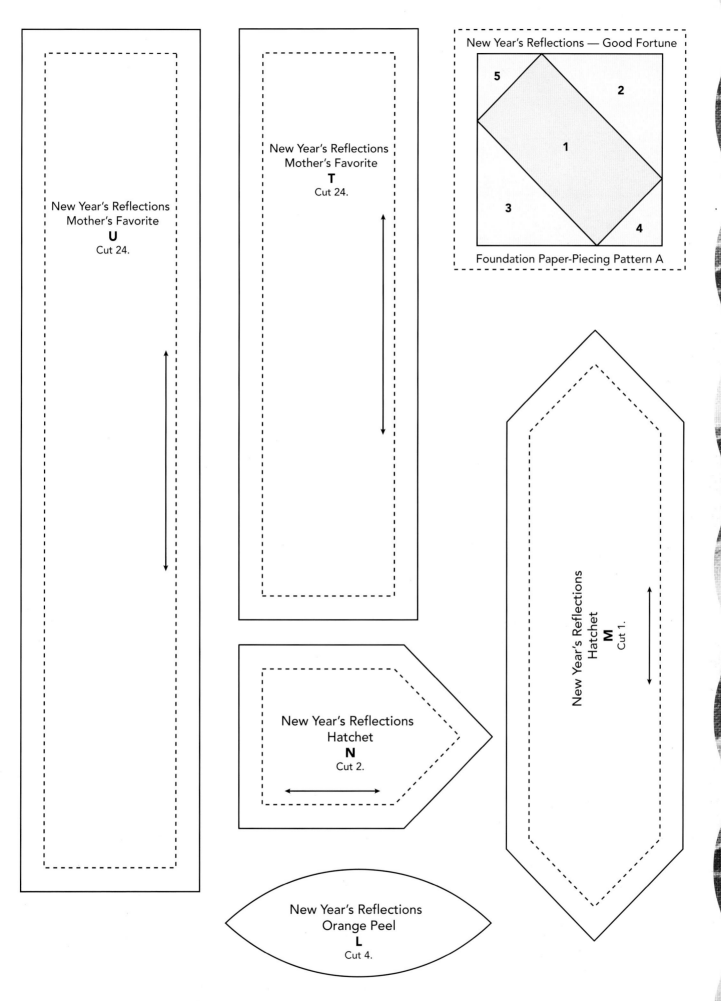

New Year's Reflections
Mother's Favorite
U
Cut 24.

New Year's Reflections
Mother's Favorite
T
Cut 24.

New Year's Reflections — Good Fortune

5

2

1

3

4

Foundation Paper-Piecing Pattern A

New Year's Reflections
Hatchet
M
Cut 1.

New Year's Reflections
Hatchet
N
Cut 2.

New Year's Reflections
Orange Peel
L
Cut 4.

Fabric requirements are based on a 42″ width. Many fabrics shrink when washed, and widths vary by manufacturer. In cutting instructions, strips are cut on the crosswise grain, unless otherwise noted.

SEAM ALLOWANCES

A ¼″ seam allowance is used throughout. It's a good idea to do a test seam before you begin sewing to check that your ¼″ is accurate.

PRESSING

In general, press seams toward the darker fabric. Press lightly in an up-and-down motion. Avoid using a very hot iron or over-ironing, which can distort shapes and blocks.

Y-SEAM CONSTRUCTION

Y-Seam construction (sometimes called "set-in" piecing) is used when 3 angled seams come together at one point. To sew these seams, do not stitch into the seam allowance at the intersection. Instead, stop and backstitch at a point ¼″ in from both edges of the patch. It helps to mark the stopping point with a dot on the wrong side of each patch.

For example, Y-seam construction is used to join a triangle between 2 diamonds, as shown in the following series of diagrams.

Mark dots on the triangle and on the diamonds.

Sew to the dot and backstitch.

Press toward the diamond.

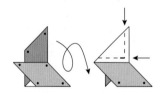

Flip the unit over and sew the other diamond to the triangle.

Sew the 2 diamonds together and backstitch.

Press.

HALF-SQUARE TRIANGLE BLOCKS

1. Draw a diagonal line from corner to corner on the wrong side of a fabric square. Place the marked square right sides together with an unmarked square.

2. Sew ¼″ away from each side of the drawn line and then cut on the drawn line to make 2 half-square triangle units. Press each unit open with the seam toward the darker fabric.

QUARTER-SQUARE TRIANGLE BLOCKS

1. Place 2 quarter-square triangles right sides together. Sew the triangles together to make a triangle pair. Press the unit open with the seam toward the darker fabric.

2. Arrange and sew 2 triangle pairs together to make a quarter-square triangle block. Press.

FOUNDATION PAPER PIECING

Once you get used to it, foundation paper piecing is an easy way to ensure that your blocks will be accurate. You sew on the side of the paper with the printed lines. Fabric is placed on the nonprinted side. With paper piecing, you don't have to worry about the fabric grain. You are stitching on paper, which stabilizes the block. The paper is not removed until after the quilt top has been constructed.

1. Trace or photocopy the number of paper-piecing patterns needed for your project.
2. Use a smaller-than-usual stitch length (1.5–1.8, or 18–20 stitches per inch) and a slightly larger needle (size 90/14). This makes the paper removal easier and will result in tighter stitches that cannot be pulled apart when you tear off the paper.
3. Cut the pieces slightly larger than necessary—about ³⁄₄˝ larger, more for triangles. They do not need to be perfect shapes—one of the joys of paper piecing!
4. Follow the number sequence when piecing. Pin piece 1 in place on the blank side of the paper, making sure you don't place the pin any-

where near a seamline. Hold the paper up to the light to make sure that the piece covers the area it is supposed to and that the seam allowance is amply covered.

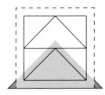

5. Fold the pattern back at the stitching line and use a small acrylic ruler and a rotary cutter to trim the fabric to a ¹⁄₄˝ seam allowance.
6. Cut piece 2 large enough to cover area 2 plus a generous seam allowance. Cut each piece larger than you think necessary; it might be a bit wasteful, but it's better than ripping out tiny stitches! Align the edge of piece 2 with the trimmed seam allowance of piece 1, right sides together, and pin. With the paper side up, sew on the line between pieces 1 and 2.

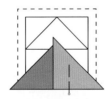

7. Open piece 2 and press.
8. Continue sewing each piece in order, being sure to fold back the paper pattern and trim the seam allowance to ¹⁄₄˝ before adding the next piece.
9. Trim all around the finished unit to the ¹⁄₄˝ seam allowance. Leave the paper intact until after the blocks have been sewn together; then carefully remove it. Creasing the paper at the seamline helps when tearing it.

Paper-Piecing Hints

When making several identical blocks, it helps to work in assembly-line fashion. Add pieces 1 and 2 to each of the blocks; then add 3, and so on.

Precutting all the pieces at once is a time-saver. Make one block first to ensure that each fabric piece will cover the area needed.

To trim the seam, place a card or an envelope along the stitching line when folding the pattern back.

Sometimes the seam allowance needs to be pressed toward the light fabric when dark and light pieces are sewn together, and the edge of the dark seam allowance might show through the light fabric. To prevent this, trim the dark seam allowance about ¹⁄₁₆˝ narrower than the light seam allowance.

PREPARATION FOR APPLIQUÉ

1. To prepare the background block for appliqué, fold it in half horizontally, vertically, and twice diagonally, pressing after each fold to mark the block's center and to create placement lines.

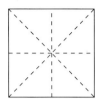

2. Using the patterns provided, trace each appliqué shape onto template plastic or freezer paper and cut out on the line. Place the appliqué templates onto the background and lightly mark their locations on the background, 1/8″ inside the sewing line.

3. Trace around the templates onto the desired appliqué fabrics, adding a scant 1/4″ seam allowance. Cut out the pieces along the pencil lines.

MACHINE APPLIQUÉ USING FUSIBLE-WEB ADHESIVE

1. Lay the fusible web sheet paper-side-up on the pattern and trace with a pencil. Trace detail lines with a permanent marker for ease in transferring to the fabric.

2. Use paper-cutting scissors to roughly cut out the pieces. Leave at least a 1/4″ border.

3. Following the manufacturer's instructions, fuse the web patterns to the wrong side of the appliqué fabrics. It helps to use an appliqué-pressing sheet to avoid getting the adhesive on your ironing board.

4. Cut out the pieces along the pencil lines. Do not remove the paper yet.

5. Transfer the detail lines to the fabric by placing the pieces on a lightbox or up against a window and marking the fabric. Use pencil for this task; the lines will be covered by thread.

6. Remove the paper and position the appliqué pieces on your project. Be sure the web (rough) side is down. Fuse in place, following the manufacturer's instructions.

MITERED BORDERS

1. Measure the length of the quilt top and add 2 times the width of your border, plus 5″. This is the length for the side borders.

2. Place pins at the centers of both side borders and at the centers of all 4 sides of the quilt top. From the center pin (on both side borders), measure in both directions and mark half of the measured length of the quilt top. Pin by matching centers and matching the marked length of the side borders to the edges of the quilt top. Sew the side borders to the sides of the quilt top. Stop and backstitch at the seam allowance line 1/4″ in from the edge. The excess length will extend beyond each edge. Press the seams toward the border.

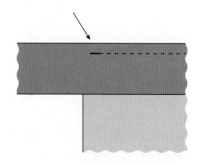

3. Determine the length needed for the top and bottom borders the same way, measuring the width of the quilt top through the center, including both side borders. Add 5″ to this measurement. Cut or piece these border strips.

4. From the center of each border strip, measure in both directions and mark half of the measured width of the quilt top on the top and bottom borders. Again, pin, sew up to the 1/4″ seamline, and backstitch. The border strips will extend beyond each end.

5. To create the miter, lay the corner right side up on the ironing board. Lay 1 border strip on top of the adjacent border strip.

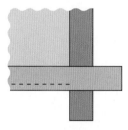

6. Fold the top border strip under itself so that it meets the edge of the other border strip at a 45° angle. Pin the fold in place.

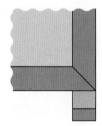

Fold under at a 45° angle.

7. Position a 90° angle triangle or ruler over the corner to check that the corner is flat and square. When everything is in place, press the fold firmly.

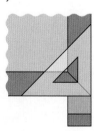

Square the corner.

8. Fold the center section of the quilt top diagonally from the corner, right sides together, and align the long edges of the borders. On the wrong side, place pins near the pressed fold in the corner to secure the border strips.

9. Beginning at the inside point, backstitch; then sew along the fold toward the outside point, being careful not to allow any stretching to occur. Backstitch at the end. Trim the excess border fabric to a ¼″ seam allowance. Press the seam open.

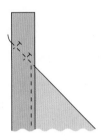

BACKING

Plan to make the backing at least 2″ larger than the quilt top on all sides. Prewash the backing fabric and trim the selvages before you sew the backing sections together. To economize, you can sew the back from any leftover fabrics or blocks in your collection.

BATTING

The type of batting to use is a personal decision; consult your local quilt shop. Cut batting approximately 2″ larger on all sides than your quilt top.

LAYERING

Spread the backing wrong side up and tape the edges down with masking tape. (If you are working on carpet, you can use T-pins to secure the backing to the carpet.) Center the batting on top of the backing, smoothing out any folds. Center the quilt top right side up on top of the batting and backing.

BASTING

If you plan to machine quilt, pin baste the quilt layers together with safety pins placed at least 3″–4″ apart. Begin basting in the center and move toward the edges first in vertical, then horizontal, rows.

If you plan to hand quilt, baste the layers together with thread using a long needle and light-colored thread. Knot one end of the thread. Using stitches approximately the length of the needle, begin in the center and move out toward the edges.

QUILTING

Whether done by hand or machine, quilting should enhance the pieced or appliqué design of the quilt. You may choose to quilt in-the-ditch, echo the pieced or appliquéd motifs, use patterns from quilting design books and stencils, or do your own free-motion quilting.

DOUBLE-FOLD STRAIGHT GRAIN BINDING (FRENCH FOLD)

1. Trim excess batting and backing from the quilt. If you want a ¼″ finished binding, cut fabric strips 2¼″ wide and sew them together end-to-end with a diagonal seam to make a continuous binding strip.

2. Press the seams open; then press the entire strip in half lengthwise with wrong sides together. With raw edges even, pin the binding to the edge of the quilt, starting a few inches from one corner and leaving the first few inches of the binding unattached. Start sewing, using a ¼″ seam allowance.

3. Stop ¼″ from the first corner and backstitch one stitch. Lift the presser foot and rotate the quilt. Fold the binding at a 45° angle so it extends straight above the quilt. Then bring the binding strip down even with the edge of the quilt. Begin sewing at the folded edge.

Sew to ¼″ from the corner.

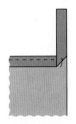

First fold for miter

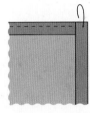

Second fold alignment. Repeat in the same manner at all corners.

4. Repeat in the same manner at all corners.

5. When you reach the beginning, fold the ending tail of the binding back on itself where it meets the beginning tail. From the fold, measure and mark the cut width of your binding strip. Cut the ending binding tail to this measurement. For example, if your binding is cut 2¼″ wide, measure and mark 2¼″ from the fold of the ending tail and cut the tail to this length.

6. Open both tails. Place 1 tail on top of the other tail at a right angle,

right sides together. Mark a diagonal line and sew on the line. Trim the seam to $1/4"$. Press open.

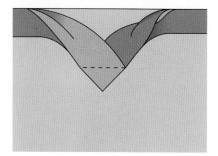

Sew the ends of the binding diagonally.

7. Finish sewing the binding to the quilt. Fold the binding over the raw edges to the quilt back and hand stitch, mitering the corners.

ABOUT *The Author*

Photo by Sigrid Estrada.

JENNIFER CHIAVERINI is the author of the best-selling Elm Creek Quilts novels, as well as *Elm Creek Quilts* and *Return to Elm Creek*, two collections of quilt projects inspired by the novels. A graduate of the University of Notre Dame and the University of Chicago, Jennifer taught writing at the Pennsylvania State University and Edgewood College. Jennifer also designs the Elm Creek Quilts fabric lines for Red Rooster Fabrics. She lives with her husband and two sons in Madison, Wisconsin.

ABOUT *The Quiltmakers*

Carol Hattan

Photo by Berniece Pepper.

CHRISTMAS MEMORIES

Carol Hattan learned to sew with her mother as a fifth grader and made her first quilt 36 years ago. A math teacher at Skyview High School in Vancouver, Washington, Carol enjoys drafting patterns in the Geometer's Sketchpad, a math program, and occasionally teaches stack-n-whack quilting classes. She belongs to the Clark County Quilters in Vancouver, Washington.

Geraldine Neidenbach

Photo by Nic Neidenbach.

MILL GIRLS

Geraldine Neidenbach of Thousand Oaks, California, became interested in quilting when her daughter encouraged her to create a sampler quilt. As a high school mathematics teacher, she appreciates the beauty of geometry in every quilt. Upon retiring after 34 years of teaching, she plans to make more quilts, travel, and spend time visiting with her two grandsons.

Heather Neidenbach

Photo by Nic Neidenbach.

ROAD TO TRIUMPH RANCH

Heather graduated from UC Santa Cruz and earned a Master of Library Science from UCLA. She has worked as an archivist for Walt Disney Imagineering and as a high school English teacher, and is currently the librarian for La Reina High School in Thousand Oaks, California. She taught herself how to quilt while in high school, and although it is a bit worse for wear, she still uses the first quilt she ever made. In addition to quilting, Heather loves to crochet, a trait she inherited from her grandmother.

Pat Morris

ARBOLES VALLEY STAR

Photo by Jerry Morris.

Pat became interested in quilting in 1991 when she found out she was to become a grandma for the first time. She took a basic quilting class intending to make just one quilt but was hooked! She loves the possibilities for creative expression that quilting provides and continues to take classes from many local and national quilting teachers.

Pat has made many quilts for loved ones, for charity, and just out of the desire to try a new technique. She eventually became a teacher herself and especially loves machine quilting and hand appliqué.

Pat now has eight grandchildren and is teaching them to quilt, too. Pat feels blessed to have found a hobby that is so satisfying and gives her a creative outlet, and she wants to pass this joy on to the next generation.

Christie Batterman

NEW YEAR'S REFLECTIONS

Photo by Christie Batterman.

Christie Batterman began quilting in her 40's, inspired by a lifelong love of fabric and art. She began sewing at a young age when her mother taught her to make dresses for her doll and progressed into making her own clothes. In 2003, she retired from Visa International, culminating a 30-year career managing software applications development. Retirement lasted only a few weeks, however, as Christie went to work part-time in a local quilt shop, expanding her quilting pursuits to include teaching and creating original designs. She is partial to colorful, contemporary quilts, which are featured in her classes. Christie and a colleague are developing a new line of quilting patterns. A native of California, Christie lives with her husband in the San Francisco Bay Area.

Sue Vollbrecht

MACHINE QUILTING

Photo by Rick Vollbrecht.

Sue has been quilting for 33 years. Her passion for quilt-making and her background in art led her to teaching, speaking engagements, and quilt pattern design. In 1997, Sue started her longarm quilting business, Quilting Memories, and quickly became known and admired for designing custom patterns to make each customer's quilt unique. Sue lives with her husband, Rick, in Monona, Wisconsin, and belongs to the Madison quilt guild, the Mad City Quilters.

Rita DeMarco

VIOLETS FOR GRETCHEN

Rita started sewing as a young girl, experimenting with home décor and garment making, but fell in love with quilting in 1980 after taking a quilting class. Since then, she has taught satin-stitch appliqué, beginning machine quilting, binding, and basic piecing. She and her daughter, Laura, are the proud owners of the oldest quilt shop in Georgia, Log Cabin Patchworks. They have successfully grown it from a 400-square-foot log cabin to over 2,000 square feet. They have designed many of their own quilts and have been featured in several prominent magazines.

Resources

For a list of other fine books from C&T Publishing,
ask for a free catalog:
C&T Publishing, Inc.
P.O. Box 1456
Lafayette, CA 94549
(800) 284-1114
Email: ctinfo@ctpub.com
Website: www.ctpub.com

For quilting supplies:
Cotton Patch
1025 Brown Ave.
Lafayette, CA 94549
(800) 835-4418 or
(925) 283-7883
Email: CottonPa@aol.com
Website: www.quiltusa.com

Note: Fabrics used in the quilts shown may not be
currently available, as fabric manufacturers keep most
fabrics in print for only a short time.

For Jennifer Chiaverini fabrics wholesale:
Red Rooster Fabrics
1359 Broadway, Ste. 1202
New York, NY 10018
(212) 244-6596

C&T Publishing's professional photography is now
available to the public. Visit us at
www.ctmediaservices.com.

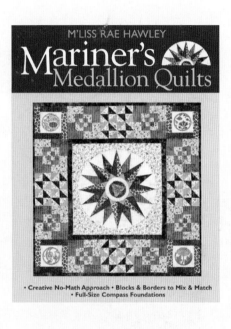

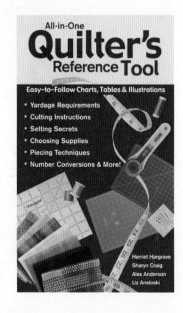